Git & GitHub Visual Guide

The Hands-on Manual

D-Libro

Table of Contents

Introduction

Version Control System (VCS) is one of the most critical tools for coding and digital application development. Git is the most commonly used version control system.

Version Control System (VCS) is one of the most critical tools for coding and digital application development. **Git** is the most commonly used version control system, created by Linus Torvalds in 2005 for the development of the Linux kernel. **GitHub** is one of the most popular Remote Repository services based on the Git platform.

In this course, we'll explain how to use Git as a version control system and how to collaborate with other developers on GitHub.

Throughout this course, you will learn:

- Key Concepts of Git and GitHub
- How to set up Git projects
- How to use Git Branches
- How to collaborate with others using GitHub repository

Chapter 1
Git & GitHub Overview

In this chapter, we'll explain the key concepts of Git and remote repository services using GitHub examples. This chapter also covers an introduction on how to start to use Git and GitHub as well as their regular workflow.

This chapter covers the following topics.

TOPICS

1. What Is Git?
2. What Is Version Control?
3. How To Save Versions in Git?
4. Collaborating on Git & GitHub - Remote Repository
5. Collaborating on Git & Git Hub - Branch
6. Git & GitHub Basic Life Cycle

What Is Git?

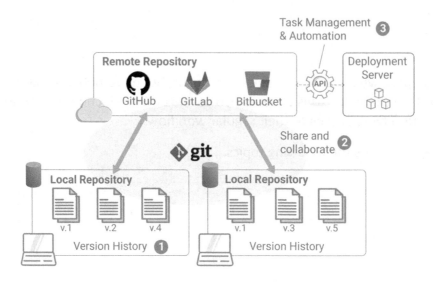

Git is a <u>free and open-source distributed version control system</u>. Git is often used with **remote repository services** such as **GitHub**, **GitLab**, and **Bitbucket**.

Git vs GitHub

Git and GitHub are often explained together, however, they are different things. <u>Git is a version control system while GitHub is a repository service provided by GitHub, Inc.</u> Typically, remote repository services also offer task management features besides collaborative coding features. For example, GitHub provides Git Issues that allow you to input tasks and share them with your team. GitHub or other remote repository services can also integrate with other services for workflow automation.

Git and remote repository services like GitHub typically provide three key features.

Key features of Git and remote repository services

1. **Version Control:** Using Git, you can <u>record</u>, <u>track,</u> and <u>retrieve</u> your coding histories.

2. **Collaborative Coding:** On Git and remote repository services, you can <u>share your code</u>, get others' codes, and <u>work as a team.</u>

3. **Task Management & Automation:** Most Git remote repository services provide additional features to <u>manage tasks</u> and <u>automate workflow</u> such as auto deployment.

What Is Version Control?

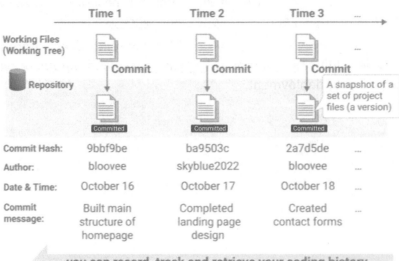

	Time 1	Time 2	Time 3
Commit Hash:	9bbf9be	ba9503c	2a7d5de
Author:	bloovee	skyblue2022	bloovee
Date & Time:	October 16	October 17	October 18
Commit message:	Built main structure of homepage	Completed landing page design	Created contact forms

you can record, track and retrieve your coding history

When coding, you need to manage several files which are dependent on one another. If you want to save different versions, you need to save entire sets of files in different directories with version names. This approach is very computer resource-consuming. Git provides solutions for this with simple Git commands.

There are two keywords to understand the Git coding history management: Repository and Commit.

Repository

A **repository** is a location where different versions of codes are stored. There are two types of repositories:

- **Local Repository:** it is installed on your local computer
- **Remote Repository**: it is usually created under a web platform such as GitHub on the Internet.

Commit

Commit creates a snapshot to record the status of coding in a repository. Only committed files are recorded in the Git log system. Committed files are saved with the following key information:

- **Commit hash**: Unique number to identify each commit
- **Author information**: Name and email address of the person who made the commit
- **Date and time**: Timing of each commit
- **Commit message**: Short title and description about the commit

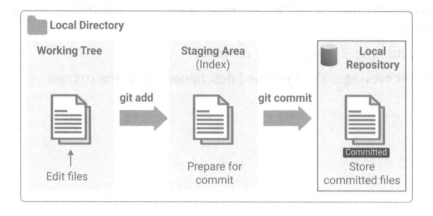

Git allows us to track all changes in our working files, however, it doesn't record every single change. Git tracks only **committed files** (a snapshot of a set of project files). This is like when we save a file on our computer as one version and save it again as another version with different file names.

Committed files are stored in a Local or Remote Repository. Through the Remote Repository, you can share your work and collaborate with others. Here we'll explain how to manage working history under a Local Repository.

Three-Stage Architecture

- **Working Tree (Working Directory)** is used to edit your working files. The files and directories that you usually see in the project directory are the *Working Tree*.

Project Directory
Working Files
...

- **Staging Area (INDEX)** is a buffer area used to prepare your working files for commit. The command to bring the working files into the *Staging Area* is **git add**. You can double-check if the files you added to the *Staging Area* are ready for commit. If the files are ready, you can commit and save them under your Local Repository. The command to commit files is **git commit**.

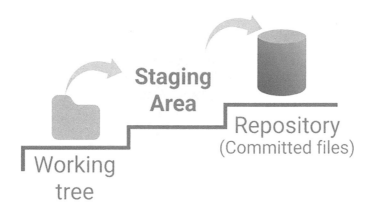

Staging Area

Repository
(Committed files)

Working tree

- **Local Repository** is a place where **committed files** are stored with version histories. By running the **git commit** command, you can commit your files in the *Staging Area* to save a version under your Local Repository. At this stage, your files are still on your computer and not accessible to others. To share the files, you need to bring the files to a **Remote Repository**, which is explained on the next page.

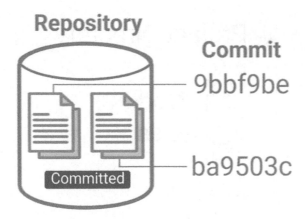

When committing files, you need to write a message describing what the commit is about: for example, *"added payment function"* or *"fixed errors"*.

When running the **git commit** command, a text editor launches automatically for writing comments. Vim text editor is the default setting typically. For the purpose of this course, Visual Studio Code will be used.

More details will be provided in **Chapter 4. Edit & Commit**.

Collaborating on Git & GitHub – Remote Repository

Collaborative coding is typically managed through a **Remote Repository**. A Remote Repository is a place where committed files are stored on the web and can be shared with others. **GitHub**, **GitLab,** or **Bitbucket** are the major remote repository services.

Interactions between a Local Repository and a Remote Repository are done through the command line on a local computer or a desktop application provided by remote repository services.

The following steps are an example flow to share project files and collaborate with a team member.

1. *Developer A* works on coding and makes the first **Commit** (saved in his Local Repository).

2. *Developer A* sends the committed files to his Remote Repository. This action is called **Push**. The command to push files is **git push**.

3. *Developer A* gives *Developer B* access to his Remote Repository.

4. *Developer B* brings the files from the Remote Repository to her local computer. When she does this for the first time, the action is called **Clone**. Clone creates the same set of files as the Remote Repository in the local computer — committed files are registered in her Local Repository and the same files are saved under the project directory. The command to clone is **git clone**.

5. *Developer B* can work on creating new lines of code and save them under her Local Repository (**Commit**).

6. *Developer B* pushes them back to Remote Repository where *Developer A* can access them.

7. *Developer A* can bring the files back to his Local Repository and his project directory. This action is called **Pull**. The command to pull files is **git pull**.

The flow above is one of the typical cases. We'll give more details about the Remote Repository in **Chapter 6. Remote Collaboration**.

Collaborating on Git & Git Hub – Branch

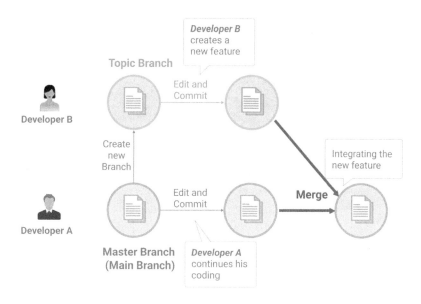

A **Branch** in Git is an independent line of development with a commit history. Each branch provides a dedicated recording space and has its own coding history (a line of commits).

Branches allow us to manage different versions of the same set of project files simultaneously. For example, one developer can work on adding a new promotion campaign feature while another developer is working on adding a new payment feature to the same web application.

Git provides a **master branch** as a default. Unless you create a new branch, all your work is done on the master branch. The branch to create a new feature is typically called a **topic branch**.

Once development is completed in a topic branch, you can **merge** it with the master branch or its parent branch.

With the branching functionality, you can efficiently collaborate with others. Or even you can utilize branches by yourself to manage versions to develop different features simultaneously.

More details of the Branch concept and operations will be explained in **Chapter 5. Work With Branches**.

master branch vs. main branch

When you create a repository from GitHub, the default branch name is **main branch**. The concepts of the master branch and the main branch are the same. Previously, the primary branch was called master branch; however, main branch as the primary branch name is becoming more mainstream.

Git & GitHub Basic Life Cycle

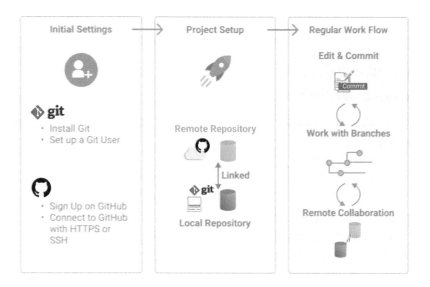

If you haven't used Git and GitHub before, you need to make the **initial settings for Git and GitHub** including sign up on GitHub and user profile settings.

You also need to set up a project with Git and GitHub. Once you complete a **basic setup for your project**, you can start to use Git and GitHub features.

There are frequently used features of Git and GitHub in the **regular workflow**.

We'll give you a high-level overview of each step in this page. The details will be explained in the following chapters.

1. Initial Settings

Before starting a project, you need to install Git software (if it's not preinstalled) and register your profile. You also need to create a GitHub account and connect your local computer with the GitHub platform by making authentication settings (HTTPS or SSH). This is a one-time operation unless you want to change your computer or your account. The details will be covered in **Chapter 2. Git & GitHub Initial Settings**.

2. Project Setup

To initiate a project with Git and GitHub, you need to create Local and Remote Repositories that will be used to save your coding and share your codes with others. At this step, you'll also establish a connection between the Local Repository and the Remote Repository. Depending on your project situation, the approach to project setup can be different. We'll explain different approaches in **Chapter 3. Project Setup**. In the chapter, we cover project setup approaches in three cases:

1. **As a project initiator (owner)**
2. **As a project member (collaborator)**
3. **As a non-project member (creating a new project using a copy of an existing project)**

Project Setup Target State

Regardless of the project setup approaches, there is a common target state of the project setup for Git and GitHub. To fully utilize Git and GitHub functionalities, you need to meet the following three conditions:

- **A Local Repository for the project** is created on your local computer
- **A Remote Repository for the project is created** on GitHub, and/or access to the project's Remote Repository is granted to the necessary project members.
- **The Local Repository and remote repository are linked** with each other so that both repositories can synchronize (typically through HTTPS or SSH connection)

Once Local and Remote Repositories are created for the project and linked, you should be able to see the same directories and files in both repositories.

The illustration below describes the target state of the Git and GitHub project setup. Once you establish this target status, you are ready to use Git and GitHub in an integrated way.

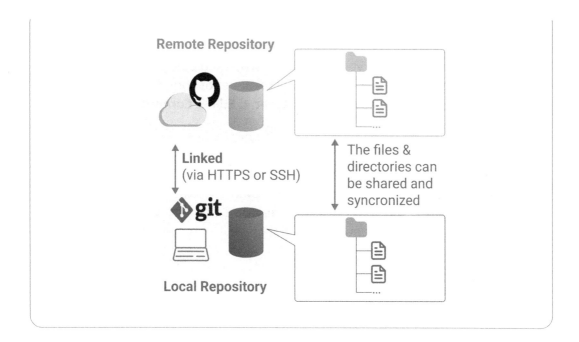

Remote Repository

Linked
(via HTTPS or SSH)

The files &
directories can
be shared and
syncronized

Local Repository

3. Regular Workflow

In the daily coding work with Git and GitHub, you are expected to use various Git commands and GitHub features on a daily basis along with the three operation areas.

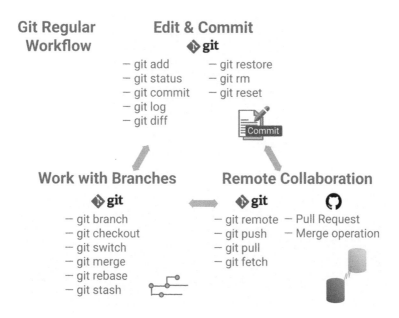

Git Regular
Workflow

Edit & Commit
git

— git add   — git restore
— git status   — git rm
— git commit   — git reset
— git log
— git diff

Commit

Work with Branches
git

— git branch
— git checkout
— git switch
— git merge
— git rebase
— git stash

Remote Collaboration
git

— git remote   — Pull Request
— git push   — Merge operation
— git pull
— git fetch

Edit & Commit

Once you launch a project, you can start to write and edit your code. You can save several versions of the code in your Local Repository by committing the codes. The details will be covered in **Chapter 4. Edit & Commit**.

Work with Branches

When you add some features while continuing to work on the main code development, you may want to manage several versions of the code. The branch functionality allows you or your team members to work on different versions of code simultaneously. The details will be covered in **Chapter 5. Work With Branches**.

Remote Collaboration

One of the key features of Git is that it allows collaboration with others. You can share your code through a Remote Repository with your team members and vice versa. The details will be covered in **Chapter 6. Remote Collaboration**.

Chapter 2

Git & GitHub Initial Settings

For programing beginners, the first hurdle to use Git and GitHub may be setting up a project environment for Git and GitHub. The approach to setting up a project environment (initial settings) differ by OS (Mac, Windows and Linux). In this chapter, we'll explain how to do the initial settings with case examples.

This chapter covers the following topics.

TOPICS

1. Git & GitHub Initial Settings Overview
2. Key Tool Preparation (1) - Mac
3. Key Tool Preparation (2) - Windows
4. Key Tool Preparation (3) - Linux Remote Server
5. Git User Settings - git config
6. Create GitHub Account
7. GitHub Access Authentication Settings
8. Generating PAT (Personal Access Token)
9. GitHub SSH Setup

There are four key steps in the Git and GitHub initial settings. In this chapter, we explain each step with several options.

Step 1. Prepare Key Tools (including Git software)

General programming tools

As Git and GitHub are coding support tools, you need to have the following basic coding tools to use Git and GitHub in your coding project. If you have coding experience, this may seem very obvious, but it may not be as obvious for beginners.

- **Command line** to execute commands and run programs
- **Text editor** to write code
- **Web browser** to access GitHub platform and to use as a UI for the program if you are developing a browser-based app

Git software

To manage your coding project with Git, you need the Git software. The Git software may already be preinstalled if you are using Mac or Linux. If you don't have it on your computer or you want to upgrade the version, you need to download and install it.

Key tool preparation approaches differ by OS (Mac, Windows, and Linux). We'll explain the different approaches on the following pages.

GitHub Desktop

If you are unfamiliar with the command line or **CUI** (Character-based User Interface), you can use Git with the **GUI** (Graphic-based User Interface). GitHub Desktop is software provided by GitHub to enable you to use Git and GitHub features without a command line. In this course, for learning purposes, we use the command line to explain how to use Git and GitHub.

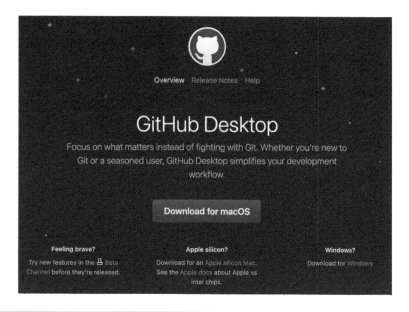

Step 2. Set up a Git user

As Git is a tool for recording coding histories including the author of edits, you need to input your basic information (i.e., username and email address). You can also register your preferred text editor which is used when you make commit messages.

Step 3. Sign up on GitHub

To use GitHub, you need to sign up for the GitHub service on its website. GitHub provides a free plan. You can start with the free plan for learning purposes.

Step 4. Connect to GitHub with HTTPS or SSH

To access GitHub from the command line, you must have proper authentication settings. Common authentication approaches for GitHub are **HTTPS** and **SSH**. **PAT (Personal Access Token)** is used for HTTPS authentication while an **SSH key pair** is used for SSH authentication.

We'll explain the above processes on the following pages.

Key Tool Preparation (1) - for Mac

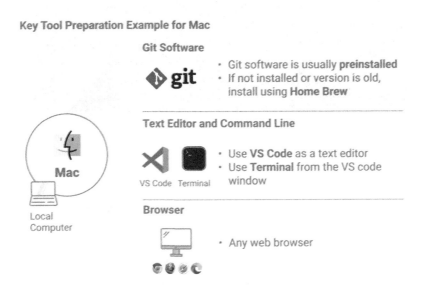

Key Tool Preparation Example for Mac

Git Software

- Git software is usually **preinstalled**
- If not installed or version is old, install using **Home Brew**

Text Editor and Command Line

- Use **VS Code** as a text editor
- Use **Terminal** from the VS code window

VS Code Terminal

Mac

Local Computer

Browser

- Any web browser

If you are using Mac, most likely Git is preinstalled on your computer. For a text editor, we use VS code throughout the course. We recommend you use it as well for practice purposes. You can also use Terminal, the command line for Mac through the VS code window.

The choice of a web browser is less critical. For our demonstration purposes, we use Chrome when we explain with examples.

In this page, we'll explain how to install the latest Git software onto a Mac computer and prepare VS code as a text editor with Terminal in the VS code window.

1. Check Git version and install Git if necessary

You can check if the Git software is installed on your computer using the command line. The command line for Mac is called Terminal. To launch Terminal, go to Launchpad and type "Terminal" in the search bar.

23

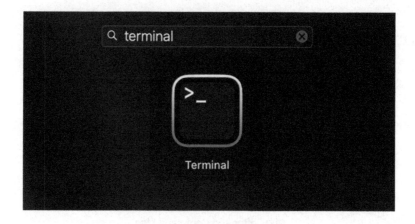

To check if Git is installed, run the command below.

Command Line - INPUT

```
git --version
```

If the command line returns its version information as shown below, Git is already installed on your computer. You can skip the following instructions.

Command Line - RESPONSE

```
git version 2.34.1
```

If Git is not installed or you want to upgrade it, follow the instructions below.

There are several options to install Git onto your computer.

The most popular one is using **Home Brew** (a package manager for macOS). Here are the steps to install Git with Home Brew:

Install Home Brew (if you don't have it on your computer)

You can check if you have Home Brew on your computer by running the command below.

Command Line - INPUT

```
brew --version
```

If Home Brew is not installed yet, run the command below. You can copy the code and paste it into the command line.

Command Line - INPUT

```
/bin/bash -c "$(curl -fsSL https://raw.githubusercontent.com/Homebrew/install/HEAD/
install.sh)"
```

Follow the instructions in the command line. To see more details about Home Brew, click on this link **Home Brew official site**[1].

Install Git

To install Git with Home Brew, run the following command

Command Line - INPUT

```
brew install git
```

To see other options to install Git onto Mac, go to this page **Git download for macOS**[2].

2. Install VS Code

For Django app coding, you can use a simple text editor and a command line; however, using an advanced code editor tool such as Visual Studio Code (VS Code), you can improve your productivity of coding. VS Code is free software provided by Microsoft. It is one of the most popular code editors among code developers. In this course, we use VS Code as a default editor.

VS Code is available on **VS Code official homepage**[3]. Here are the steps to install VS Code on Mac.

---

1 https://brew.sh/
2 https://git-scm.com/download/mac
3 https://code.visualstudio.com/download

1. Go to the official site. Select your OS and follow the instructions to install VS Code.

2. Go to the Downloads folder.

If you are using Chrome, you may see that a zip file is downloaded. Double-click the zip file to uncompress the downloads folder. If you are using Safari, the uncompressed file is already created in the Downloads folder.

Drag and drop the **Visual Studio Code.app** icon onto the **Application** folder.

3. Open Launchpad from the Dock. You can find the Visual Studio Code app.

4. To create an icon in the Dock, drag and drop the Visual Studio Code app on to the Dock from Launchpad.

5. Going forward, you can open the VS Code from the Dock.

3. Launch Terminal with VS code

To open Terminal in the VS code window, click on Terminal in the **top menu bar** and select **New Terminal**.

You can see that Terminal is opened at the bottom of the VS code window.

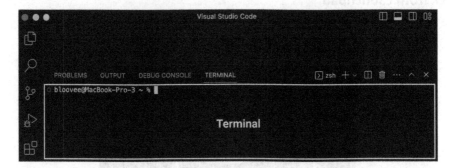

Mac Settings

If you are using Mac, it's helpful for you to know the following basic settings.

1. Show hidden files and directories

Mac (**Finder**) doesn't show hidden files and directories by default. When you want to show them, press the ⬆ shift + ⌘ command + . keys. To hide them, you can press the same keys again.

2. Show file and directory path

Unlike Windows Explore, Mac's Finder may not show the path to a file or directory by default. To show the file path, press the ⌥ option + ⌘ command + P keys. To hide it, you can press the same keys again.

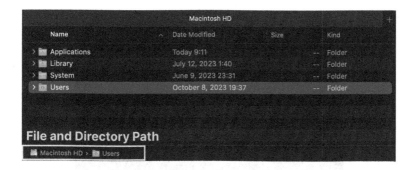

3. Show file extension

You may encounter a situation in which file extensions are hidden. To see file extensions of all files,

- Select **Finder** on the top menu bar and click on **Preferences...**

- **Under the** Advanced **tab, check** Show all filename extensions

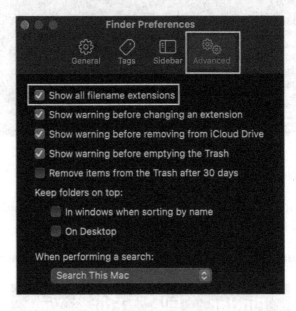

Note: Even though you uncheck **Show all filename extensions**, you may still see file extensions. This is because the file extension setting is not set as hidden. To see the individual file profile and settings, select the file that you want to check and press the ⌘ command + i keys.

Key Tool Preparation (2) - Windows

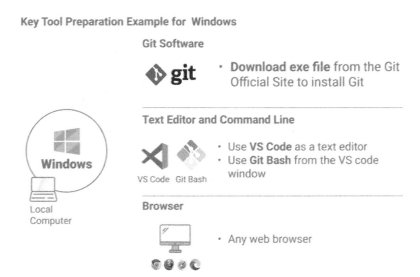

Key Tool Preparation Example for Windows

Preparing the Git environment in Windows is slightly complex. You need to install the Git software with several initial settings. For Windows, **Powershell** is usually used as a command line, but Git provides a Unix-based command line called **Git Bash**. In this course, we assume that Windows users are using Git Bash. For the text editor, we use VS code as an example. You can open Git Bash using VS code so that you can use a command line and text editor in the same application.

The choice of a web browser is less critical. For our demonstration purposes, we use Chrome when we explain with examples.

In this page, we'll explain how to install the latest Git software onto a Windows computer and prepare VS code as a text editor with Git Bash in the VS code window.

1. Install Git

To install Git onto Windows computer, follow the steps below.

Download Git installation package

Go to this site **Git download for Windows**[4] and click on "**Click here to download**".

---

4 https://git-scm.com/download/windows

The Git installation package will be downloaded onto your computer.

Open the downloaded .exe file and follow the installation instructions.

First, you'll be asked to allow the app to make changes to your device. To start the installation process, click on **Yes**.

Once the installation process is initiated, you'll need to confirm many initial settings.

Click on the **Next** buttons in the following pop-up windows. You can also click on the Next button for the default editor setting without changing the selection. We can change the default editor to Visual Studio Code later.

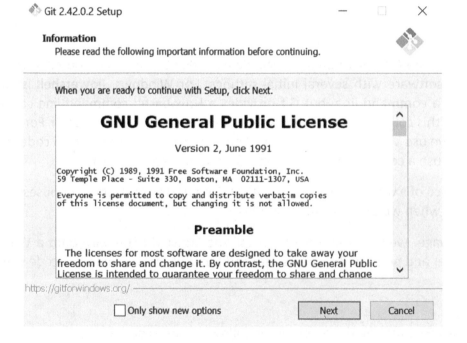

Git 2.42.0.2 Setup — □ X

Select Destination Location
Where should Git be installed?

Setup will install Git into the following folder.

To continue, click Next. If you would like to select a different folder, click Browse.

C:\Program Files\Git   Browse...

At least 321.5 MB of free disk space is required.
https://gitforwindows.org/

Back   Next   Cancel

Git 2.42.0.2 Setup — □ X

Select Components
Which components should be installed?

Select the components you want to install; clear the components you do not want to install. Click Next when you are ready to continue.

- [ ] Additional icons
  - [ ] On the Desktop
- [x] Windows Explorer integration
  - [x] Open Git Bash here
  - [x] Open Git GUI here
- [x] Git LFS (Large File Support)
- [x] Associate .git* configuration files with the default text editor
- [x] Associate .sh files to be run with Bash
- [ ] Check daily for Git for Windows updates
- [ ] (NEW!) Add a Git Bash Profile to Windows Terminal

Current selection requires at least 321.5 MB of disk space.
https://gitforwindows.org/

Back   Next   Cancel

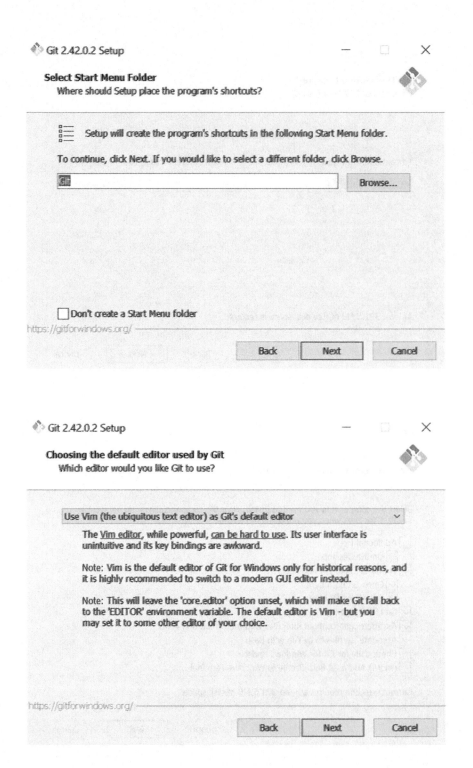

For the initial branch name setting, you can change the default branch name to **main**; however, for practice purposes and to avoid complexity, select the first option. Continue clicking on the **Next** buttons in the following pop-up windows.

Adjusting the name of the initial branch in new repositories
What would you like Git to name the initial branch after "git init"?

○ **Let Git decide**

Let Git use its default branch name (currently: "master") for the initial branch
in newly created repositories. The Git project intends to change this default to
a more inclusive name in the near future.

○ **Override the default branch name for new repositories**

NEW! Many teams already renamed their default branches; common choices are
"main", "trunk" and "development". Specify the name "git init" should use for the
initial branch:

main

This setting does not affect existing repositories.

https://gitforwindows.org/

Git 2.42.0.2 Setup   —   ☐   ✕

Adjusting your PATH environment
How would you like to use Git from the command line?

○ **Use Git from Git Bash only**

This is the most cautious choice as your PATH will not be modified at all. You will
only be able to use the Git command line tools from Git Bash.

◉ **Git from the command line and also from 3rd-party software**

(Recommended) This option adds only some minimal Git wrappers to your
PATH to avoid cluttering your environment with optional Unix tools.
You will be able to use Git from Git Bash, the Command Prompt and the Windows
PowerShell as well as any third-party software looking for Git in PATH.

○ **Use Git and optional Unix tools from the Command Prompt**

Both Git and the optional Unix tools will be added to your PATH.
Warning: This will override Windows tools like "find" and "sort". Only
use this option if you understand the implications.

https://gitforwindows.org/

Back	Next	Cancel

Git 2.42.0.2 Setup   —   □   ✕

Choosing the SSH executable
Which Secure Shell client program would you like Git to use?

⊙ **Use bundled OpenSSH**

    This uses ssh.exe that comes with Git.

○ **Use external OpenSSH**

    NEW! This uses an external ssh.exe. Git will not install its own OpenSSH
    (and related) binaries but use them as found on the PATH.

https://gitforwindows.org/ ─────────

| Back | Next | Cancel |

Git 2.42.0.2 Setup   —   □   ✕

Choosing HTTPS transport backend
Which SSL/TLS library would you like Git to use for HTTPS connections?

⊙ **Use the OpenSSL library**

    Server certificates will be validated using the ca-bundle.crt file.

○ **Use the native Windows Secure Channel library**

    Server certificates will be validated using Windows Certificate Stores.
    This option also allows you to use your company's internal Root CA certificates
    distributed e.g. via Active Directory Domain Services.

https://gitforwindows.org/ ─────────

| Back | Next | Cancel |

Git 2.42.0.2 Setup — □ ✕

Configuring the line ending conversions
How should Git treat line endings in text files?

◉ **Checkout Windows-style, commit Unix-style line endings**

Git will convert LF to CRLF when checking out text files. When committing text files, CRLF will be converted to LF. For cross-platform projects, this is the recommended setting on Windows ("core.autocrlf" is set to "true").

○ **Checkout as-is, commit Unix-style line endings**

Git will not perform any conversion when checking out text files. When committing text files, CRLF will be converted to LF. For cross-platform projects, this is the recommended setting on Unix ("core.autocrlf" is set to "input").

○ **Checkout as-is, commit as-is**

Git will not perform any conversions when checking out or committing text files. Choosing this option is not recommended for cross-platform projects ("core.autocrlf" is set to "false").

https://gitforwindows.org/ ─────────────────────────

| Back | Next | Cancel |

Git 2.42.0.2 Setup — □ ✕

Configuring the terminal emulator to use with Git Bash
Which terminal emulator do you want to use with your Git Bash?

◉ **Use MinTTY (the default terminal of MSYS2)**

Git Bash will use MinTTY as terminal emulator, which sports a resizable window, non-rectangular selections and a Unicode font. Windows console programs (such as interactive Python) must be launched via `winpty` to work in MinTTY.

○ **Use Windows' default console window**

Git will use the default console window of Windows ("cmd.exe"), which works well with Win32 console programs such as interactive Python or node.js, but has a very limited default scroll-back, needs to be configured to use a Unicode font in order to display non-ASCII characters correctly, and prior to Windows 10 its window was not freely resizable and it only allowed rectangular text selections.

https://gitforwindows.org/ ─────────────────────────

| Back | Next | Cancel |

Git 2.42.0.2 Setup — □ ✕

Choose the default behavior of `git pull`
What should `git pull` do by default?

⦿ **Default (fast-forward or merge)**

This is the standard behavior of `git pull`: fast-forward the current branch to
the fetched branch when possible, otherwise create a merge commit.

○ **Rebase**

Rebase the current branch onto the fetched branch. If there are no local
commits to rebase, this is equivalent to a fast-forward.

○ **Only ever fast-forward**

Fast-forward to the fetched branch. Fail if that is not possible.

https://gitforwindows.org/

| Back | Next | Cancel |

Git 2.42.0.2 Setup — □ ✕

Choose a credential helper
Which credential helper should be configured?

⦿ **Git Credential Manager**

Use the cross-platform Git Credential Manager.
See more information about the future of Git Credential Manager here.

○ **None**

Do not use a credential helper.

https://gitforwindows.org/

| Back | Next | Cancel |

Git 2.42.0.2 Setup — □ ✕

Configuring extra options
Which features would you like to enable?

☑ **Enable file system caching**

File system data will be read in bulk and cached in memory for certain operations ("core.fscache" is set to "true"). This provides a significant performance boost.

☐ **Enable symbolic links**

Enable symbolic links (requires the SeCreateSymbolicLink permission). Please note that existing repositories are unaffected by this setting.

https://gitforwindows.org/

[Back] [Next] [Cancel]

Finally, click on the **Install** button.

Git 2.42.0.2 Setup — □ ✕

Configuring experimental options
These features are developed actively. Would you like to try them?

☐ **Enable experimental support for pseudo consoles.**

This allows running native console programs like Node or Python in a Git Bash window without using winpty, but is unfortunately not quite stable yet.

☐ **Enable experimental built-in file system monitor**

(NEW!) Automatically run a built-in file system watcher, to speed up common operations such as `git status`, `git add`, `git commit`, etc in worktrees containing many files.

https://gitforwindows.org/

[Back] [Install] [Cancel]

Check **Launch Git Bash** and click on **Finish**.

You can check what Git Bash looks like.

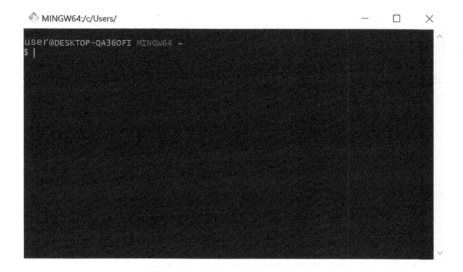

2. Install VS Code

VS Code is available on **VS Code official homepage**[5]. Here are the steps to install VS Code on Mac.

Go to the official site. Select Windows to download VS Code.

---

5 https://code.visualstudio.com/download

Open the downloaded .exe file and follow the installation instructions.

After opening the downloaded .exe file, agree to the software license.

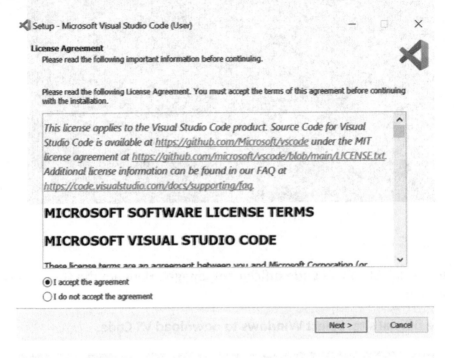

Click on the **Next** buttons again in the following pop-up windows.

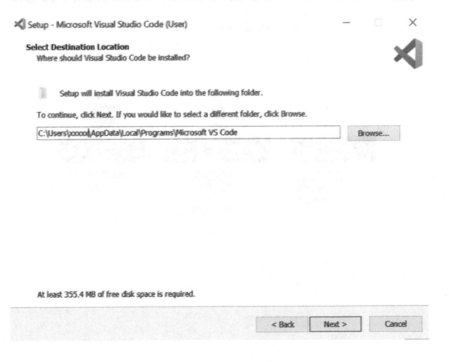

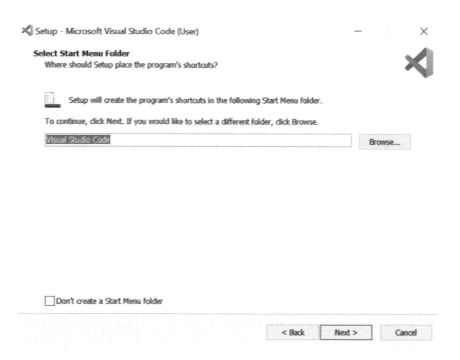

For the additional tasks, check all the items so that you can open VS code in various ways.

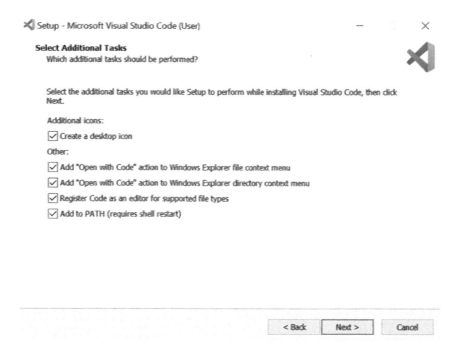

Click on the **Install** button and complete the installation.

Setup - Microsoft Visual Studio Code (User)   —   □   ×

Ready to Install
Setup is now ready to begin installing Visual Studio Code on your computer.

Click Install to continue with the installation, or click Back if you want to review or change any settings.

> Destination location:
>   C:\Users\xxxxx\AppData\Local\Programs\Microsoft VS Code
>
> Start Menu folder:
>   Visual Studio Code
>
> Additional tasks:
>   Additional icons:
>   Create a desktop icon
>   Other:
>   Add "Open with Code" action to Windows Explorer file context menu
>   Add "Open with Code" action to Windows Explorer directory context menu
>   Register Code as an editor for supported file types
>   Add to PATH (requires shell restart)

                                                    [< Back] [**Install**]   [Cancel]

Setup - Microsoft Visual Studio Code (User)   —   □   ×

Installing
Please wait while Setup installs Visual Studio Code on your computer.

Extracting files...
C:\Users\tomoo\AppData\Local\Programs\Microsoft VS Code\Code.exe

                                                                        [Cancel]

Setup - Microsoft Visual Studio Code (User)   —   ▢   ✕

**Completing the Visual Studio Code
Setup Wizard**

Setup has finished installing Visual Studio Code on your computer. The
application may be launched by selecting the installed shortcuts.

Click Finish to exit Setup.

☑ Launch Visual Studio Code

Finish

3. Set Git Bash as the default command line and open it in VS Code

Set Git Bash as the default command line

As Git Bash is not a default command line for Windows, you need to check the settings.

In the VS code window, click on the **settings icon** at the bottom left corner and select **Settings**.

45

Type *terminal.integrated.default profile: windows.* and select **Git Bash** in the drop-down list.

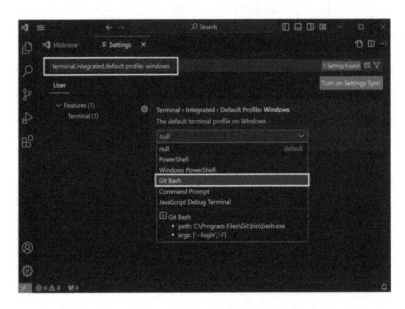

Open Git Bash in VS Code

To open Git Bash in the VS code window, click on **Terminal** in the top menu bar and select **New Terminal**.

You can see that Git Bash is opened at the bottom of the VS code window.

Windows Settings

If you are using Windows, it's helpful for you to know how to show extensions as well as hidden files and directories.

To show them, open Windows Explorer and check the following items on the top bar (Ribbon).

- **File name extensions**
- **Hidden items**

Key Tool Preparation (3) – Linux Remote Server

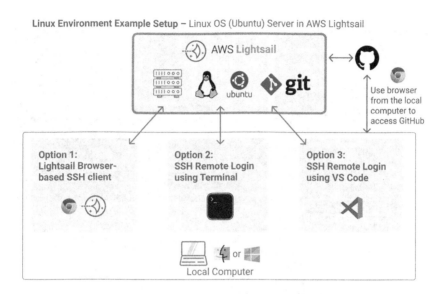

Linux Environment Example Setup – Linux OS (Ubuntu) Server in AWS Lightsail

When you launch a new app, you may need to manage Git in the remote server connected to your GitHub account. As Linux OS is often used for servers, we'll explain how to set up the remote server environment.

As Git is usually pre-installed on Linux, the focus of this topic page is more on remote environment setup. If this topic is not relevant to your situation, skip this page.

Accessing the GitHub platform is still done through a web browser on your local computer; however, there are several options to access your remote server and utilize Git on your remote server.

In this page, we'll introduce three options using Linux OS installed on the AWS Lightsail instance.

- **Option 1**: Lightsail Browser-based SSH client
- **Option 2**: SSH Remote Login using Terminal (for Mac OS)
- **Option 3**: SSH Remote Login using VS Code

Option 1: Lightsail Browser-based SSH client

1. Set up an AWS Lightsail instance to launch a Linux server

If you don't have an AWS account, create it first. From the AWS console service menu, select *Compute* and go to *Lightsail*.

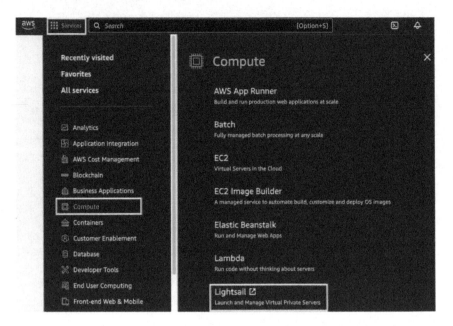

From the Lightsail console, we'll create a new instance using **Ubuntu 22.04 LTS.**

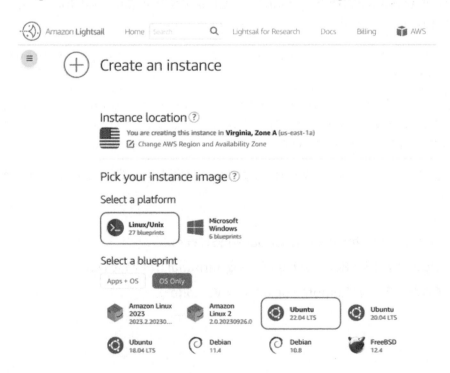

Select the cheapest option.

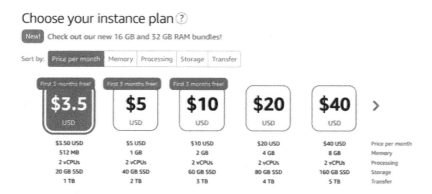

Change the instance name to **GitHub-Practice** and create an instance.

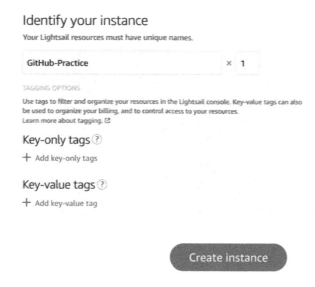

After a few minutes, the new instance will be created.

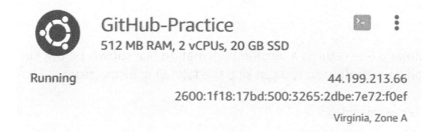

2. Check if Git is installed

Once the instance is created, click on the command line icon to launch a browser-based SSH client.

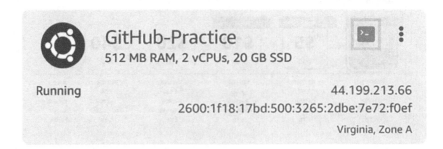

You can use it as a command line for Linux OS.

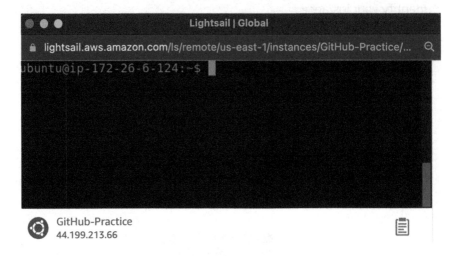

To check if Git is installed, run the command below.

Command Line - INPUT

```
git --version
```

If the command line returns a version information like shown below, Git is already installed on your computer. You can skip the following instructions.

Command Line - RESPONSE

```
git version 2.34.1
```

If Git is not installed or you want to upgrade it, follow the instructions below.

3. Update or install Git

A typical approach to install Git onto Linux computers is through the Linux command line.

Installation commands differ by Linux distributions. If you are using Debian/Ubuntu, you can use the **apt-get** command.

Command Line - INPUT

```
sudo apt-get update
sudo apt-get install git
```

For other Linux distributions, please check this link **Git download for Linux**[6].

Option 2: SSH Remote Login using Terminal (for Mac OS)

If you are using Mac OS, you can access the AWS Lightsail instance using your Terminal. There are two approaches depending on how to generate SSH keys. Check the following topics under the Linux OS Introduction course to learn how to set up SSH remote login using Terminal.

SSH Remote Login (1) - Use Key Pair Generated by Server[7]

SSH Remote Login (2) - Use Key Pair Generated by Client[8]

Creating the SSH config file is also helpful to speed up the remote login process.

SSH Config File[9]

The approaches to check, update, or install Git are the same as the ones we explained in option 1.

Note: If you are using Windows, you can use PowerShell to access the AWS Lightsail instance. The approaches to set up the SSH remote login are the same as the ones using Terminal.

---

6 https://git-scm.com/download/linux
7 https://d-libro.com/topic/ssh-remote-login-1-use-key-pair-generated-by-server
8 https://d-libro.com/topic/ssh-remote-login-2-use-key-pair-generated-by-client
9 https://d-libro.com/topic/ssh-config-file

Option 3: SSH Remote Login using VS Code

You can also use VS Code for SSH remote login to access a remote server. There are VS Code extensions to support the remote login. Check the following topics under the Linux OS Introduction course to learn how to set up the SSH remote login using VS Code.

SSH Remote Login with Visual Studio Code[10]

The approaches to checking, updating, or installing Git are the same as the ones we explained in option 1.

---

10 https://d-libro.com/topic/ssh-remote-login-with-visual-studio-code

Git User Settings – git config

```
$ git config
```

Username setting
```
$ git config --global user.name your username
```

e-mail setting
```
$ git config --global user.email your email address
```

Text editor setting
```
$ git config --global core.editor "your editor path -- wait"
```

Check registered setting
```
$ git config --global --list
```

Unset registered setting
```
$ git config --global --unset unset item name (e.g., user.name)
```

The next step after Git installation is registering your user profiles on Git. In this page, we'll cover the following items relating to the initial Git configurations.

1. Register your user name and email address
2. Register a text editor
3. Check configured settings
4. Clear configured settings

1. Register your username and email address

Git tracks who made changes. To track change history with editor information, you need to register your **username** and **email address** first before using Git.

To register a username, type and run the following code in your command prompt.

Command Line - INPUT

```
git config --global user.name [your username]
```

To register an email address, run the following code.

```
git config --global user.email [your email address]
```

Note: The --**global** option is used to apply settings to the user of the computer. If you don't use this option, the settings will be registered only to the Local Repository you are working on.

2. Register a text editor

When you run the **git commit** command, you need to add notes in the text editor. The default text editor is normally **Vim**, however, using a more advanced text editor increases your productivity. Some text editors can be integrated with GitHub to build more seamless operations.

To register your text editor, run the following command.

```
git config --global core.editor "[editor path] --wait"
```

In this course, we'll use Visual Studio Code (VSC). **code** is the editor path of VSC. To use the path, you need to register it on your computer when installing VSC.

3. Check user settings

To confirm the setting, you need to run the following code.

```
git config --global --list
```

4. Unset user settings

The settings you made can be modified. Use the --**unset** option to clear your settings and register new settings. For example, if you want to change your username in the Git configuration, run the following code to unset your username.

```
git config --global --unset user.name
```

Practice

Objective:
Set up a Git user

1. Open the command line in VS Code

Open VS Code and open a new terminal. The image below is an example of Mac OS.

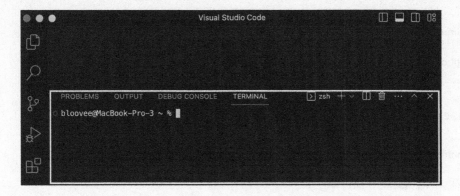

2. Register your username and email address

To register a username and an email address, run the following code in the terminal. We'll be using a *bloovee* account as an example in this course.

Command Line - INPUT

```
git config --global user.name bloovee
git config --global user.email bloovee@example.com
```

You can see if your username and email address are successfully registered by running the command below.

Command Line - INPUT

```
git config --global --list
```

You'll see the status of the username and email settings like the one below.

```
user.name=bloovee
user.email=bloovee@example.com
```

3. Register your text editor

Next, register your text editor. In this case, we'll be registering Visual Studio Code (VSC). **code** is the editor path of VSC.

```
git config --global core.editor "code --wait"
```

Check the status by running the **git config --global --list** command

```
git config --global --list
```

you'll see that the editor is also registered as shown below.

```
user.name=bloovee
user.email=bloovee@example.com
core.editor=code --wait
```

4. Unset user settings

Deregister username, email, and text editor by running the following command.

```
git config --global --unset user.name
git config --global --unset user.email
git config --global --unset core.editor
```

Check the status by the **git config --global --list** command, and you'll see that all the settings are cleared.

Local configuration

You can also set different user profiles for each project. To set local configurations, run the **git config** command without any options or with the **--local** option. You need to run the command in the project directory where your Git Local Repository exists. How to create a Local Repository will be explained in the next chapter.

The next step for the initial setup is to create an account on a remote repository service. To use GitHub, you need to sign up for the GitHub service on its website. GitHub provides a free plan. You can start with the free plan for learning purposes. Here we'll explain how to set up a GitHub account.

1. Go to the GitHub official site and click "Sign up" on the top right

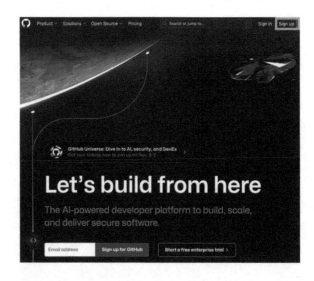

GitHub official site[11]

2. Enter your email, password, and username

You'll also need to answer some questions.

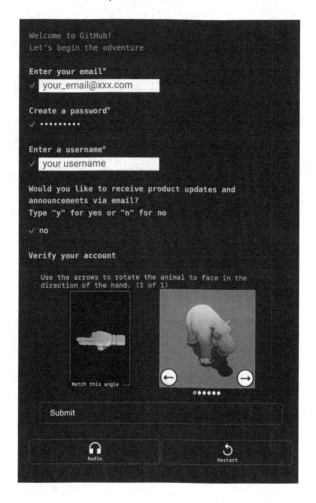

_____

11 https://github.com/

3. Verify your email account

After you register your username, email address, and password, a pass code will be sent to your email address. You will need to enter the pass code on the site.

4. Choose your account plan

Usually, the free plan is enough for learning purposes.

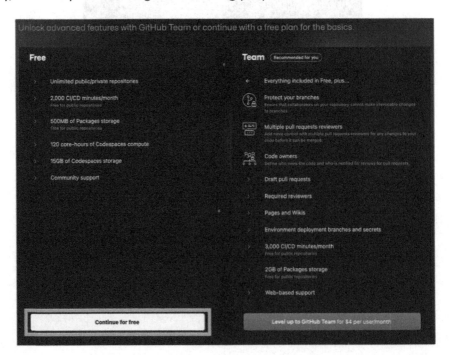

5. Optional: set up your user icon

A user icon is auto-generated as an initial setting. You can replace it with your own icon or picture. To set up your user icon,

Click on the **user icon(avatar)** on the top right

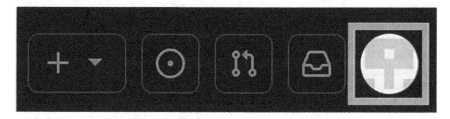

Select Your profile

Click on the **large user icon(avatar)** on the left

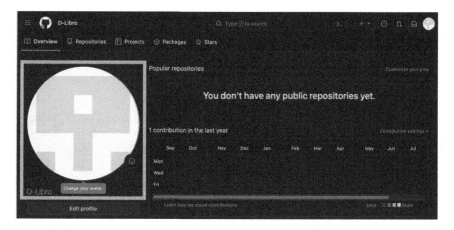

Click on the **Edit** button on the user icon (avatar) and select **Upload a photo...**

You can upload your avatar in the PNG, JPG, or GIF format. It may take a few minutes to replace the icon images.

GitHub Access Authentication Settings

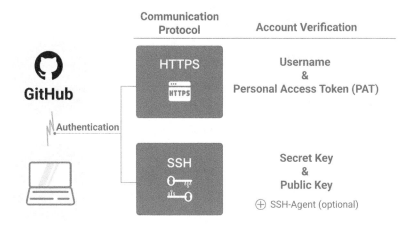

You can access Remote Repositories on GitHub from the command line in two ways: **HTTPS** and **SSH**. When you clone the repository or establish remote settings, you can choose the method of authentication by your URL choice. Git provides different URLs of a Remote Repository for HTTPS and SSH.

HTTPS

HTTPS uses username and **PAT (Personal Access Token)** as an account verification approach. Previously, we used GitHub password instead of PAT. To enhance security, GitHub introduced PAT. You need to generate PAT prior to using HTTPS. HTTPS is considered faster than SSH and you can usually work with all repositories on GitHub over HTTPS, even if you are behind a firewall or proxy. The way to generate PAT is explained on the next page.

SSH

SSH uses **a pair of secret key and public key**. You need to generate a key pair and upload the public key onto the GitHub account site. SSH can be slower than HTTPS, however, you can add several settings using the config file. Firewalls and proxies might refuse to allow SSH connections. In that case, you need to add proxy server settings in the Git system. The way to add SSH settings in GitHub will be explained later.

Generating PAT (Personal Access Token)

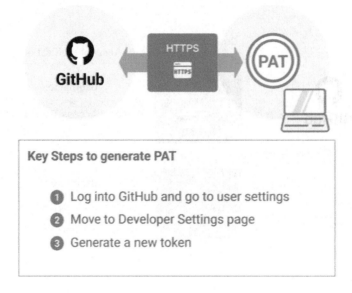

To establish HTTPS connection, you'll need **PAT (Personal Access Token)**. There are two types of PAT: **Tokens (classic)** and **Fine-grained tokens** (beta version). When you use the Fine-grained tokens, you can add more detail settings. For the beginner practice purposes, we'll explain how to set up PAT using the classic one.

1. Log into GitHub and go to user settings

Go to the GitHub website (**GitHub**[12]), click on your icon, and press the Settings button.

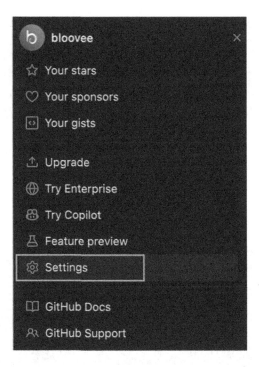

2. Move to Developer Settings page

Go to the bottom of the left sidebar and select **Developer settings**.

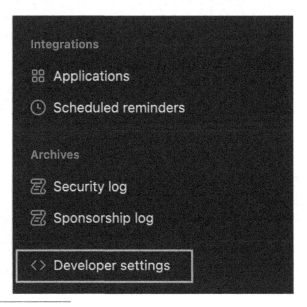

---

12 https://github.com/

3. Generate a new token

Select Tokens (classic) **under** Personal access tokens **and press the** Generate new token button. **Select** Generate new token (classic).

Add **Note** (describe what the token is for) and set **Expiration**. After the token expires, you need to generate another token.

In the **Select scopes** section, you need to check **repo** to get access to your Private Remote Repositories. You can add other scopes later when required.

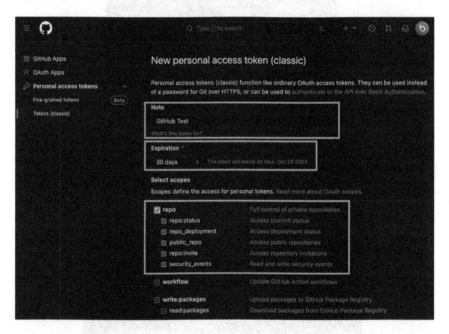

Press the **Generate token** button.

When a new token is successfully generated, you'll see your PAT. Make sure you'll copy it and save it somewhere as it won't be shown again.

When PAT is used?

PAT is used when you establish an HTTPS connection to your Remote Repository. To establish HTTPS connections going forward, go to your repository on GitHub and press the **Code** button. Make sure to select the **HTTPS** tab to get the URL for HTTPS. (the URL for SSH is different). This URL is used when you run the clone, push, or pull command.

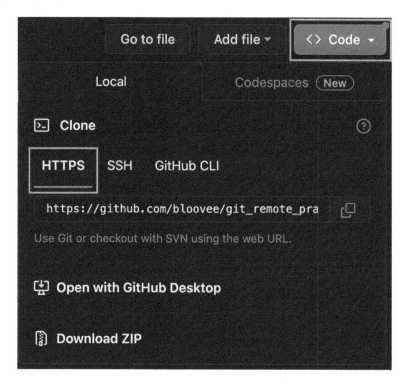

When you clone, push, or pull, you'll be asked for your username and password. You need to use PAT instead of the GitHub password. Previously, it was a GitHub password, however, GitHub changed the rule to strengthen the security level. How to establish an HTTPS connection will be explained in the later chapters along with the key git commands: **git clone**, **git remote**, **git push,** and **git pull**.

GitHub SSH Setup

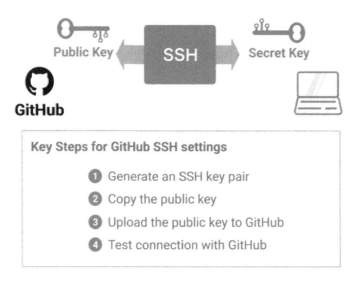

To establish an SSH connection, you need an SSH key pair (a private key and a public key) and upload the public key to the GitHub platform.

One of the benefits of SSH connection is the easiness of connecting to the GitHub repository. If you skip setting a **passphrase** or use **ssh-agent**, you don't need to type a passphrase every time you connect with a GitHub repository.

There are several approaches in SSH settings. In this topic, we'll explain the most simple one. In the next topic, we'll explain more advanced settings using ssh-agent and customizing the SSH key file path. If you want to pursue the advanced settings, you can skip this page and go to the next page.

In the approach that we'll explain in this page, there are four key steps:

1. Generate an SSH key pair
2. Copy the public key
3. Upload the public key to GitHub
4. Test connection with GitHub

Generate an SSH key pair

The first step in SSH setup is to generate a new SSH key pair. To generate it, run the command below.

File path

When running the command, you'll be asked to enter the file in which to save the key. You can specify a file path or you can just hit the enter key to skip. If you skip the setting, the key pair will be created in the default path.

Passphrase

When running the command, you'll be asked to set a **passphrase**. This passphrase gives another layer of security. If you don't want to type a passphrase every time you connect to GitHub, you can skip setting a passphrase although the security level decreases.

To set a passphrase, type your passphrase twice. Save the passphrase as the passphrase is used when you establish ssh connection.

When the command is executed, the files of the public and private keys are generated under the *.ssh* directory under your user home directory. As it is a hidden directory, you need to change the settings to show the hidden directory. For Mac OS, press the shift + command + . keys.

> ### Command Options
>
> **-t option** is to set security type. **rsa** has mainly been used; however, GitHub recommends **ed25519** now for better security. If you are using a legacy system that doesn't support the Ed25519 algorithm, you can use rsa. The command to generate an SSH key is the one below.
>
> ```
> ssh-keygen -t rsa -b 4096 -C "your email address"
> ```
>
> Check this link **GitHub - Generating a new SSH key**[13] for more details.
>
> **-C option** is to overwrite a comment in the key. As the default comment is username@hostname, it is good to overwrite to avoid disclosing your hostname. Typically, an email address is used for the comment.

Copy the public key

To add the public key to GitHub in the next step, you need to copy it first.

cat command

Show public key content by running the **cat** command.

```
cat file_path
```

Copy the displayed public key and go to the next step.

pbcopy or clip command

Alternatively, you can directly copy the content of the file without displaying the file content by using the **pbcopy** command for Mac,

```
pbcopy < file_path
```

or the **clip** command for Windows.

```
clip < file_path
```

---

13 https://docs.github.com/en/authentication/connecting-to-github-with-ssh/generating-a-new-ssh-key-and-adding-it-to-the-ssh-agent

For Linux, a similar command may not be available by default unless you install it.

Upload the public key to GitHub

You need to add the copied public key to the GitHub account setting page by conducting the following actions.

1. Go to the **GitHub website**
2. Click **your icon**
3. Press the **Settings** button
4. Select **SSH and GPG keys** on the left side bar
5. Press **New SSH key** button
6. Set **Title** and paste the **public key**

Test connection with GitHub

You can check if you can connect with GitHub using the **ssh** command with the **-T** option.

```
ssh -T git@github.com
```

You'll see a message confirming that you've been successfully authenticated.

Practice

Set up an SSH connection to GitHub

In this practice example, we use *bloovee* as a username and *bloovee@example. com* as an email address. You need to change them to your own username and email.

Note: The file path shown in the command line response is an example based on Mac OS.

1. Generate an SSH key pair

Run the **ssh-keygen** command

Command Line - INPUT

```
ssh-keygen -t ed25519 -C "bloovee@example.com"
```

After running the command, you'll be asked to indicate the file path to save the file.

Command Line - RESPONSE

```
Generating public/private ed25519 key pair.
Enter file in which to save the key (/Users/bloovee/.ssh/id_ed25519):
```

The default SSH key path

The default SSH key file paths are slightly different by OS as the OS user home directory paths are different.

Windows: **/C/Users/bloovee/.ssh/id_ed25519**

Linux: **/home/bloovee/.ssh/id_ed25519**

To create an SSH key pair in the default file path, hit the `enter` key. You'll be asked for a passphrase.

Command Line - INTERACTIVE

```
Enter passphrase (empty for no passphrase):
Enter same passphrase again:
```

To create the key pair without a passphrase, hit the (enter) key two times. A key pair is saved under the file path displayed. You'll see the following response in your command line.

You can confirm that the two files are generated in the *.ssh* directory under your home directory. The *.ssh* directory is a hidden directory. If you cannot see it, you need to make hidden directories and files visible. For Mac, press the (shift) + (command) + (.) keys.

2. Copy the public key

cat command

Show public key content by running the **cat** command.

Copy the displayed public key and go to the next step.

pbcopy or clip command

Alternatively, you can directly copy the content of the file without displaying it by using the **pbcopy** command for Mac, or the **clip** command for Mac

For Mac:

Command Line - INPUT

```
pbcopy < ~/.ssh/id_ed25519.pub
```

For Windows:

```
clip < ~/.ssh/id_ed25519.pub
```

3. Upload the public key to GitHub

Go to the GitHub website, click **your icon,** and press the **Settings** button.

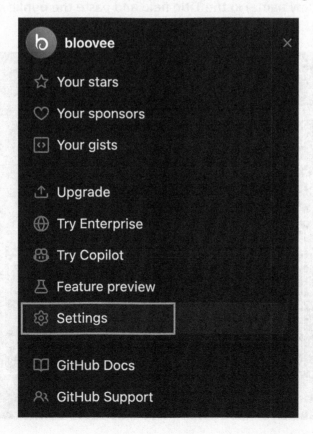

Select the **SSH and GPG keys** on the left sidebar and press the **New SSH key** button.

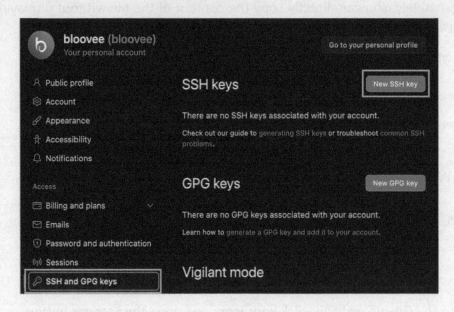

Fill title name (any name) in the **Title** field and paste the public key information in the **Key** field.

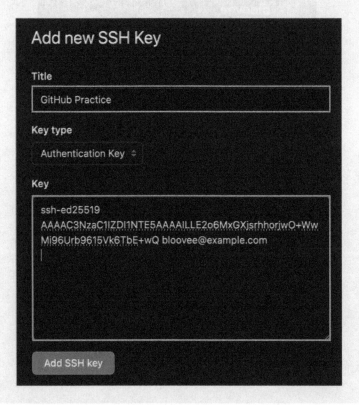

You'll see that the public key is registered.

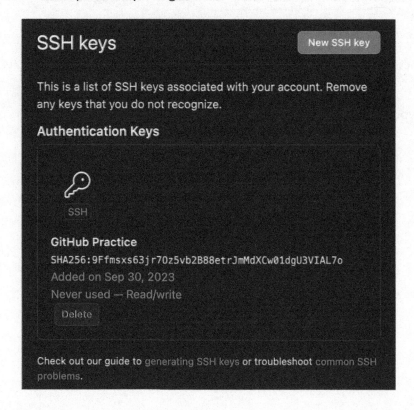

4. Test connection with GitHub

Run the **ssh** command with the GitHub URL.

Command Line - INPUT

```
ssh -T git@github.com
```

You may get the following message if you are connecting to GitHub first time.

Command Line - INTERACTIVE

```
The authenticity of host 'github.com (20.27.177.113)' can't be established.
ED25519 key fingerprint is SHA256:+DiY3wvvV6TuJJhbpZisF/zLDA0zPMSvHdkr4UvCOqU.
This key is not known by any other names
Are you sure you want to continue connecting (yes/no/[fingerprint])?
```

Type **yes** and hit the ⬛enter⬛ key

If the test connection is successful, you'll see the message below.

Command Line - RESPONSE

Hi bloovee! You've successfully authenticated, but GitHub does not provide shell access.

Now, you are ready to connect to GitHub with SSH.

## Chapter 3

Git & GitHub Project Setup

To initiate a project with Git and GitHub, you need to create Local and Remote Repositories that will be used to save your coding and share your codes with others.

At this step, you'll also need to connect the Local Repository with the Remote Repository. <u>Depending on your project situation, the project setup approach can be different.</u>

In this chapter, we'll explain the project setup approaches in the three cases below:

- **Case 1: As a project initiator (owner)**
- **Case 2: As a project member (collaborator)**
- **Case 3: As a non-project member (creating a new project using a copy of an existing project)**

Topics covered in this chapter are the following.

TOPICS

1. Three Cases in Git & GitHub Project Setup
2. Git & GitHub Project Setup Overview in Different Cases
3. Building Remote Collaboration Practice Environment
4. Project Initiator - Key Steps To Launch Git Project
5. Project Initiator - Create Local Repository (git init)
6. Project Initiator - Make the First Commit
7. Project Initiator - .gitignore File
8. Project Initiator - Create Remote Repository
9. Project Initiator - Link Between Remote and Local Repositories (git remote add)
10. Project Initiator - Upload Local Repository to Remote Repository (git push)

---

11. Project Initiator - Grant Remote Repository Access to Project Members

12. Project Member - Start Project As Collaborator

13. Project Member - Create Copy of Project Code on Local Computer (git clone)

14. Non-Member - Start Project With Replica of Existing Repository (Fork)

15. Fork vs. Clone

Three Cases in Git & GitHub Project Setup

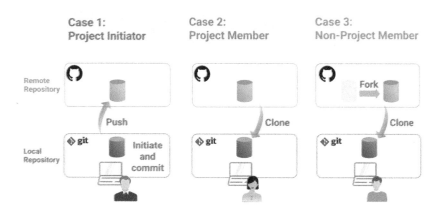

Typically, there are three cases to launch a Git project depending on who initiates it and becomes the owner of the Remote Repository. Depending on your role in the project, the approaches to the Git & GitHub project setup differ. Before we explain how to set up a project for each case, we'll briefly explain what the three cases are.

Case 1. Project initiator (owner)

If you want to initiate a Git project yourself, you need to create a Local Repository on your local computer with the **git init** command. Then, you can develop code and commit it to keep recording the code version history using Git. Once the code is ready to share with others, you can create a Remote Repository on the GitHub platform and transfer the code to it. After you give your project member (collaborator) access to the repository, your project member can get the code from the repository.

Case 2. Project member (collaborator)

If you join a project as a project member (called **collaborator** in the GitHub terminology), you don't need to create a Git Local Repository by the **git init** command. Once you get access to the Remote Repository from the repository owner, you can create a copy of the project code on your local computer by running the **git clone** command. When you clone the code, a Local Repository is also created on your local computer, and the code and commit history are stored in the repository.

Case 3. Non-project member

Even though you are not a member of the project (not designated as a project collaborator), if the Remote Repository is publically available, you can create a replica of the project code and you can start a project using the code. The action to create a replica of an existing repository called **Fork**. In this case, you'll become the owner of the forked repository.

Git & GitHub Project Setup Overview in Different Cases

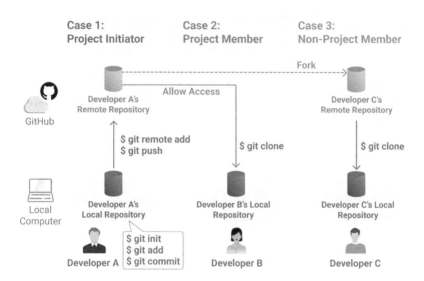

As explained, depending on your role in the project, the approach for the Git & GitHub project setup is different. In this page, we'll explain the key steps of Git & GitHub project setup for each case.

Case 1. Project initiator (owner of the Remote Repository)

In this case, you launch a new Git project from your local computer by initiating a Local Repository yourself. As a project initiator, you also need to set up a Remote Repository for the project to share project documents with your project members. There are four key steps until the project documents are ready to be shared on GitHub.

Step 1. Create a Git Local Repository

As a project initiator, the first thing you need to do is to initiate a Local Repository for the project. **git init** is the command to create a new Local Repository.

Step 2. Develop code and commit it to the Git Local Repository

Until you start to store or share documents through Remote Repositories on GitHub, you work on the project with the Git system on your local computer. We'll explain a typical workflow of Git local operations in the next chapters (Chapter 5: Edit &

Commit, Chapter 6: Work with Branches). In this chapter, we'll cover this step only briefly.

Step 3. Set up a GitHub Remote Repository

When you want to share your project documents on GitHub, you need to create a Remote Repository on GitHub. Creating a Remote Repository is done through the GitHub web platform.

Step 4. Share project documents in the GitHub Remote Repository

In this step, you prepare to share project documents through the Remote Repository. Before uploading your project documents, you need to establish a link between your Local Repository and your Remote Repository by running the **git remote add** command. To upload the committed documents, run the **git push** command. When the documents are successfully uploaded, they are ready to be shared with others. To share the documents, you need to invite your project members to the Remote Repository and give them access to your Remote Repository.

Case 2. Project member (collaborator of the Remote Repository)

In this case, a Remote Repository with project documents is already prepared by the project owner. To join and start the project, you need to follow the two steps below.

Step 1. Get access to the Remote Repository

If there is a Remote Repository of the project you are trying to participate in, what you need to do is get access to the Remote Repository where you can obtain the project documents.

Step 2. Clone the Remote Repository

Once you get access to the Remote Repository, you can start to get project documents by running the **git clone** command. The **git clone** command brings the project documents onto your local computer while creating a Local Repository. The command also establishes a link between the Local Repository and the Remote Repository so that you can start to interact with the Remote Repository from the command line on your computer.

Case 3: Non-project member (without collaborator access to the original Remote Repository)

In this case, a Remote Repository with project documents is available on the GitHub platform but you may not have collaborator access to the project. Even though you don't have collaborator access, you can initiate a new project using the code in the repository by creating a replica of the repository. There are two key steps for you to follow.

Step 1. Create a replica of an existing Remote Repository (Fork)

As GitHub is an open platform, you can access many repositories created by someone else. You may want to leverage an existing repository to start your new project. In this case, you need to **Fork** the existing repository. The fork feature creates a replica of the existing repository under your GitHub account. Once you fork a repository, you'll become the owner of the forked repository.

Step 2. Clone the Remote Repository

As in Case 2, you can bring the project documents to your local computer by running the **git clone** command.

Note: Even if you have collaborator access to the repository or you are the owner of the repository, you can also execute a fork to use the repository for different objectives.

Case Study

In this section, we'll explain the flow of the project setup with three developer role examples.

Roles in the case study

Developer A: The original initiator of the project

Developer B: A team member (collaborator) supporting *Developer A* on the project

Developer C: An independent developer who wants to leverage existing codes to launch a new project

---

The following explanation assumes that all developers already have Git software installed on their computers and they already signed up GitHub account and completed PAT or SSH settings.

Developer A's point of view

The objective of *Developer A* is to start to collaborate with *Developer B* for the project. He needs to upload his code to his Remote Repository and share it with *Developer B*.

1. *Developer A* already has some lines of code under a project directory.
2. To record version history, he creates a Git Local Repository under the project directory by running the **git init** command.
3. Once the Local Repository is initiated, he commits the latest code by running the **git add** and **git commit** commands.
4. To prepare to share the project document, *Developer A* creates a Remote Repository under his GitHub account.
5. To upload his codes to the Local Repository, he creates a link between the Local Repository and the Remote Repository by running the **git remote add** command.
6. Once the Remote Repository and the Local Repository are linked, he can upload his code by running the **git push** command.
7. Finally, he needs to allow *Developer B* to access his Remote Repository. This operation is done on the GitHub web platform.

Developer B's point of view

The objective of *Developer B* is to get access to *Developer A*'s Remote Repository for the project and bring the project directory to her local computer to start the project.

1. When *Developer A* gives *Developer B* permission to access his Remote Repository, an email is sent by GitHub. What *Developer B* needs to do first is to accept the invitation.
2. Next, she needs to link the Remote Repository with her Local Repository and bring the project directory to her local computer by running the **git clone** command. After cloning the repository, she is ready to collaborate with *Developer A*.

Developer C's point of view

The objective of *Developer C* is to launch a project based on *Developer A*'s existing work. Here we assume that *Developer A*'s Remote Repository is a public repository.

1. The first thing *Developer C* needs to do is to **Fork** the repository. The fork feature creates a replica of an existing repository; however, it is no longer linked to the original repository. Fork operation is done through the GitHub web platform. After he creates a new Remote Repository by fork, the new repository is owned by him and he can freely edit the code in his repository.

2. To edit the code, he needs to bring the project directory to his local computer by running the **git clone** command.

Practice Setting

In this course, we'll use the three GitHub accounts below to demonstrate practice examples so that you can clearly understand different roles.

Role	Icon	GitHub Username
Developer A		bloovee
Developer B		sky-blue2022
Developer C		ocean-blue2022

Remote Collaboration Practice Environment
(Example of using one computer)

Repository Owner's environment   Collaborator's environment

Access

Developer A's GitHub
Account and Repository

Developer B's
GitHub Account ④

Linked   Linked

git   git

Developer A's
project directory and
Local Repository

Developer A's   Developer B's
browser   browser

Developer B's
project directory and ②
Local Repository

Developer A's OS user   ③   Developer B's OS user ①

If you want to fully understand the remote collaboration approach with Git and GitHub, you need to understand at least two different user perspectives:

- **The owner of the Remote Repository**
- **A collaborator of the Remote Repository**

For effective learning on Git and GitHub, creating a practice environment with multiple users is important. There are three approaches you can try:

- **Option 1: Practice with someone else**. By switching between the project owner and project member roles, you can practice both of them.

- **Option 2: Use two computers**. If you have two computers, you can experience each role using different computers. In this option, you need to create two GitHub accounts for the project owner role and project member role.

- **Option 3: Create two user accounts for OS**. Also, in this option, you need to create two GitHub accounts for the project owner role and project member role.

If you are practicing on your own and don't have two computers, a realistic option is option 3.

Here we'll explain how to create a remote collaboration practice environment on your own with a single computer.

In a real-life situation, different developers use different computers, different email addresses, and different GitHub accounts as illustrated in the main figure. The ideal practice environment imitates these real-life situations.

Note: There is a case of a non-collaborator but if you understand the two perspectives, understanding the non-collaborator's point of view should be straightforward.

In this page, we'll cover the following points to establish the remote collaboration practice environment described in the main figure.

1. **Create two user accounts on your computer** (the primary OS user account and the secondary OS user account)
2. **Prepare a project directory and VS Code with the command line for each user**
3. Prepare a browser for each user
4. Prepare GitHub accounts for each user

As we haven't explained a project-specific setup, the following approaches will be explained in the next chapter

- How to create a Local Repository
- How to create a Remote Repository
- How to create a link between the Local Repository and the Remote Repository
- How to grant the Remote Repository access

Practice

Objective:
Set up the remote collaboration practice environment

In this practice section, we'll explain the approach using the Mac OS example. Regardless of the OS you use, you can usually create more than one user account on your computer.

For Windows OS, there are additional explanations at the bottom of this section.

1. Creating two users on your computer

Open **System Preferences**.

Select **Users & Groups**.

Unlock to make changes.

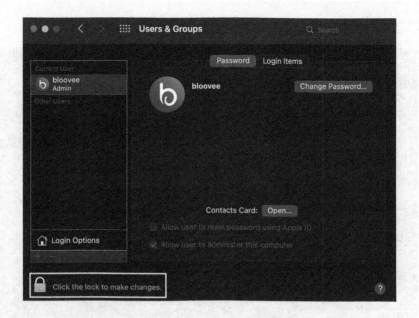

Enter your password to unlock.

Click on the + button.

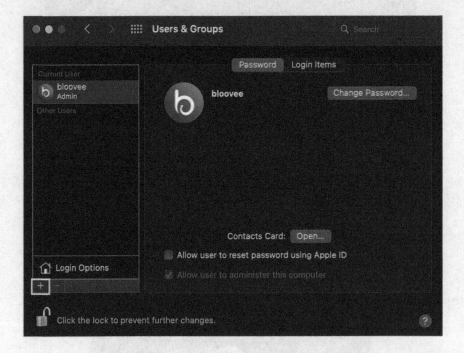

Type your user name under the **Full Name** section. **Account Name** is automatically filled. Account Name is used for the home folder name that is shown in the command line.

Once you create a new account, you can also customize the user icon.

To switch the user, lock the screen and select Switch User.

Now, you can log into the system with the new account.

2. Prepare a project directory and VS Code with the command line for each user

Next, you need to create another local environment with a text editor and command line.

Locate the VS Code App and register it in the Dock

As you have already installed VS Code, you should be able to access VS Code. In the **Launchpad**, search VS Code.

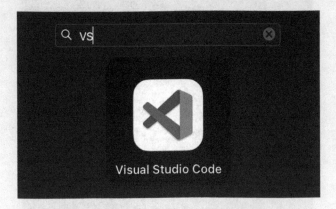

Bring it to the **Dock** for easy access.

Create a main project directory in each OS account

Create a main project directory for practice for each account. For example, we use the following project directory names.

- *Dev_A_bloovee* for *Developer A*'s project directory
- *Dev_B_skyblue* for *Developer B*'s project directory

Create the directory under each user's home directory. You can create it using the OS GUI (Graphic User Interface) or using a command line.

Option 1: Use GUI to create the project's main directory

For Developer A (Project Owner Role)

Create a new directory using your main OS user account used for the project owner role (Developer A). The screenshot below shows the directory structure including the directories that will be created in the later chapters. At this point, create the project's main directory (e.g., *Dev_A_bloovee*) under your primary OS user account directory.

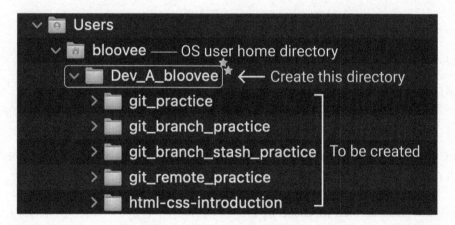

For Developer B (Project Member Role)

Create a new directory using your secondary OS user account used for the project member (collaborator) role (Developer B). The screenshot below shows the directory structure including the directories that will be created in the later chapters. At this point, create the project's main directory (e.g., *Dev_B_skyblue*) under your secondary OS user directory.

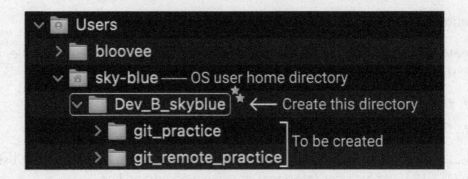

Option 2: Use the command line to create the project's main directory

If you use a command line, run the following commands from each user account. To run the command from each account, you need to switch the user in the OS. You can use account names of your choice.

For Developer A (Project Owner Role)

Run the following commands from your main OS user account that is used for the project owner role (Developer A).

Command Line - INPUT (Developer A)

```
cd ~
mkdir Dev_A_bloovee
cd Dev_A_bloovee
pwd
```

After running the commands, you can confirm your current working directory path as shown below.

Command Line - RESPONSE (Developer A)

```
/Users/bloovee/Dev_A_bloovee
```

For Developer B (Project Member Role)

Run the following commands from your secondary OS user account that is used for the project member (collaborator) role (Developer B).

```
cd ~
mkdir Dev_B_skyblue
cd Dev_B_skyblue
pwd
```

After running the commands, you can confirm your current working directory path as shown below.

Command Line - RESPONSE (Developer B)

```
/Users/bloovee/Dev_B_skyblue
```

Set up VS Code and the command line

For the secondary account, we haven't used VS Code yet. To open the project directory using VS Code, drag & drop the directory onto the VS Code icon.

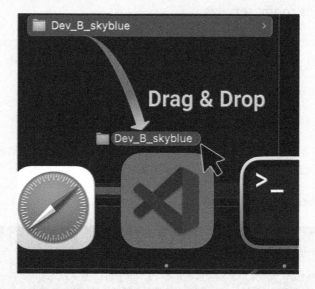

Open a command line in VS Code by selecting **New Terminal** under the **Terminal** menu on the top menu bar. You'll see that your account name is shown in the command line and the project main directory is set as the current working directory.

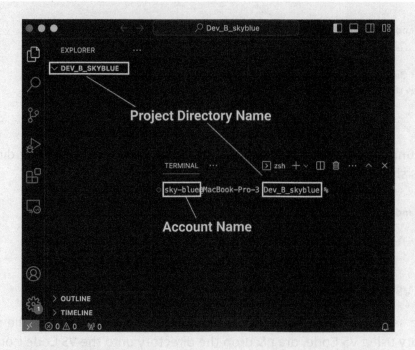

Project Directory Name

Account Name

Complete the git config settings

As you created a new OS user account, you need to do the git config settings for the user as well. Check this link for the **git config** command **Git User Settings - git config**[1]

3. Prepare a browser for each user

As GitHub uses a browser cache for the user login, it is also better to set up two browsers. If you use Chrome, you need two Gmail accounts.

Developer A's browser example

---

1 https://d-libro.com/topic/git-user-settings-git-config

Developer B's browser example

4. Prepare GitHub accounts

Create another GitHub account using your second email. If you already have two accounts, for example, a private account and a work account, you don't need to create a new one.

For your secondary account, check **Create GitHub Account**[2].

Here are examples of GitHub accounts used in the practice sections.

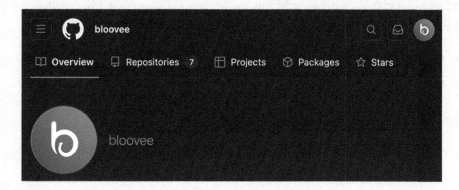

Developer A's GitHub account example

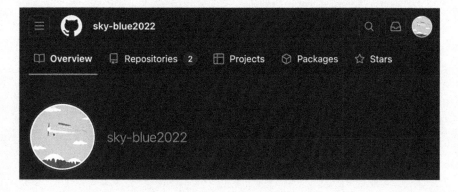

2 https://d-libro.com/topic/create-github-account

Developer B's GitHub account example

For the new account, you also need to prepare a communication protocol (HTTPS or SSH) to access GitHub from your command line. Refer to the following pages for the setup.

- **Generating PAT (Personal Access Token)**[3]
- **GitHub SSH Setup**[4]

---

3 https://d-libro.com/topic/generating-pat-personal-access-token
4 https://d-libro.com/topic/github-ssh-setup

Project Initiator – Key Steps To Launch Git Project

Project Initiator

			Key Commands	Platform
Step 1		Create Git local repository	$ git init	git

Step 2	comit	Develop code and commit it to local repository
		– Edit project files and make a commit
		– Utilize .gitignore file
			$ git add
			$ git commit
			$ git status
			$ git log
				git

Step 3		Set up remote repository – Create new repository – Invite collaborators	(Operations on GitHub web platform)	
Step 4		Share project documents – Link between remote and local repositories – Upload project documents	$ git remote add $ git push	git

We have already explained the key steps of Git & GitHub project setup for the three cases. From this page onwards, we are zooming into the project initiator's case. Here are the key points of each step. We'll explain each step on the following pages.

Step 1. Create a Git Local Repository

- To record version history, you need to create a Local Repository in your project directory.
- By running the **git init** command in your project directory, you can create a Local Repository.

Step 2. Develop code and commit it to the Git Local Repository

- To create a version record, you need to make a commit. If you haven't committed your code yet, you cannot transfer your code to your GitHub Remote Repository.
- In this chapter, we'll explain how to make the first commit with a brief explanation of the four basic key commands (**git add, git commit, git status, git log**).
- There are some files or directories that you don't want to share with others. To exclude those files or directories, you can use the **.gitignore** file.

Step 3. Set up a GitHub Remote Repository

- We already explained the initial settings of GitHub in the previous chapter. In the previous chapter, we only covered general settings. To use GitHub for a specific project, you need to create a Remote Repository for the project.

- You can create a Remote Repository on the GitHub web platform.

Step 4. Share project documents in the GitHub Remote Repository

- Before sharing project documents, you need to establish a link between remote and Local Repositories by registering a URL of the remote repository in the Local Repository. The command to establish the link is **git remote add**.

- Once the Local Repository and the Remote Repository are linked, you can upload project documents by running the **git push** command.

- To share the documents, you need to invite your project members to the Remote Repository and give them access to your Remote Repository.

Project Initiator – Create Local Repository (git init)

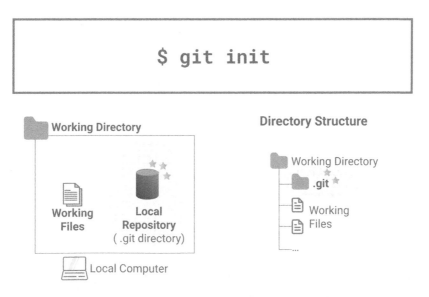

The first step to launch a Git project is to run the **git init** command. The command will create a Local Repository in the current working directory.

This command doesn't require any options or arguments. You need to simply run the following command in the directory where you want to generate a new project.

Command Line - INPUT

```
git init
```

After running the command, a Local Repository is created under a hidden directory named *.git*. If you cannot see it, you need to make hidden directories and files visible. For Mac, press the  keys.

Practice

Developer A (Project Owner Role)

Objective:
Create a Git Local Repository

1. Setup a practice project directory and file for this chapter

Target directory and file structure

For this practice, we'll use the following directory and file. The directory and file will be used throughout the practices in this chapter and the next chapter.

- Practice project directory: *git_practice*
- *Practice file:* git_practice.html

The screenshot below is the <u>target directory structure</u> example based on Mac OS.

Create the practice project directory and file

Open the project's main directory (e.g., *Dev_A_bloovee*) with VS Code. You can use drag & drop to open the directory.

After opening the project's main directory with VS Code, open a new terminal in the VS Code window.

Make sure that your current working directory in the command line is the project's main directory (e.g., *Dev_A_bloovee*)...

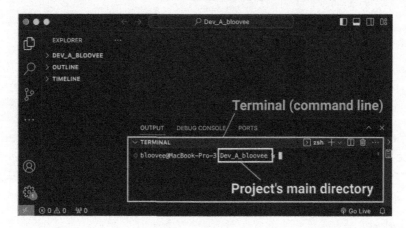

...and run the commands below to create the directory and file.

Command Line - INPUT

```
mkdir git_practice
cd git_practice
touch git_practice.html
```

2. Create a Local Repository

To create a Local Repository, run the **git init** command in the *git_practice* directory.

Command Line - INPUT

```
git init
```

You'll see the message as shown below. On Windows, you may not see the hint messages.

Command Line - RESPONSE

```
hint: Using 'master' as the name for the initial branch. This default branch name
hint: is subject to change. To configure the initial branch name to use in all
hint: of your new repositories, which will suppress this warning, call:
hint:
hint: git config --global init.defaultBranch <name>
hint:
hint: Names commonly chosen instead of 'master' are 'main', 'trunk' and
hint: 'development'. The just-created branch can be renamed via this command:
hint:
hint: git branch -m <name>
Initialized empty Git repository in /Users/bloovee/git_practice/.git/
```

After running the command, one hidden directory named **.git** is created. This is the place where the Local Repository is created.

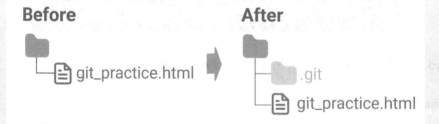

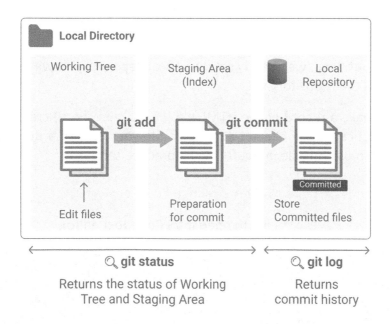

Although we'll provide more details about Git operations on the local computer in the next chapter, in this chapter, we'll briefly explain the four key commands that will help launch a project and make the first commit.

- **git add**: with this command, you can add files to the *Staging Area*, where you can prepare and check files to register in your Local Repository.

- **git commit**: with this command, you can register files in your Local Repository. Once the files are registered by this command, you can retrieve the saved version of the set of files anytime.

- **git status**: with this command, you can see the status of the *Working Tree* and the *Staging Area*. This status lets you see which changes have been staged, which haven't, and which files aren't being tracked by Git.

- **git log**: with this command, you can see commit histories in a Local Repository.

The following practice helps you understand the four key commands.

Practice

Developer A (Project Owner Role)

Objective:
Make the first commit

On the previous page, we already set up a Local Repository, however, nothing is recorded in the repository yet.

Here, we'll make a record of the HTML file (*git_practice.html*) created in the previous practice. As we haven't edited the file yet, prepare a dummy code first. We'll also use this file in the following practice sections.

1. Prepare an HTML file for this practice

Select the *git_practice.html* file to open it VS Code text editor.

Edit the HTML file like the following, and save the file. You can use shortcuts to save the file (⌘ + S for Mac, Ctrl + S for Windows).

git_practice.html

```html
<!doctype html>
<html lang="en">
<head>
    <style>
        h1 {
            color: blue;
            font-size:80px
        }
    </style>
</head>
<body>
    <h1>Hello World!</h1>
</body>
```

2. Check how the file is tracked by the Git system

Although the file is saved under the *git_practice* directory. It is still NOT recorded under the Git repository yet. To check the status, you can run the **git log** command. Open the command line in VS Code and run the command.

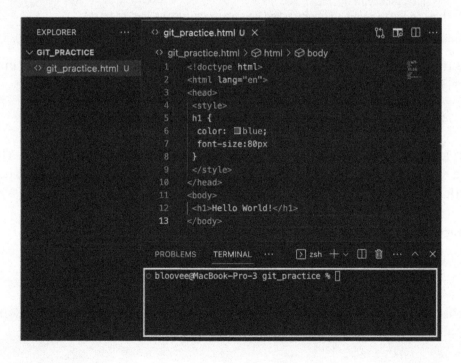

Command Line - INPUT

```
git log
```

You can see the message explaining that nothing has been committed yet like the one below.

```
fatal: your current branch 'master' does not have any commits yet
```

Also, if you run the **git status** command, you can see that there are untracked files.

Command Line - INPUT

```
git status
```

Command Line - RESPONSE

```
No commits yet
Untracked files:
    (use "git add ..." to include in what will be committed)
        git_practice.html
nothing added to commit but untracked files present (use "git add" to track)
```

This means the file exists in the *Working Tree*, however, it's not registered in the Local Repository or the *Staging Area*.

3. Register the file in the Staging Area

To register the file in the Local Repository, first run the **git add** command. Make sure you are in the *git_practice* directory in your command line, and use . (period) to add all the files under the current directory.

Command Line - INPUT

```
git add .
```

At this stage, the files are not registered in the Local Repository yet. Check how the file is tracked by the Git system by running the **git status** command.

Command Line - INPUT

```
git status
```

Command Line - RESPONSE

```
On branch master
No commits yet
Changes to be committed:
    (use "git rm --cached ..." to unstage)
        new file: git_practice.html
```

4. Register the file in the Local Repository

Run the **git commit -m** *"the first commit"* command to register the files in the Local Repository. You can add comments to the commit using the **-m** option.

If you don't put this option, a text editor is launched to add comments. In that case, you need to type your comments in the text editor and save it. After closing the editor, you can come back to the command line.

Command Line - INPUT

```
git commit -m "the first commit"
```

Command Line - RESPONSE

```
[master (root-commit) 651e510] the first commit
 1 file changed, 13 insertions(+)
 create mode 100644 git_practice.html
```

Run the **git log** command again to check the commit status. Now you can see that the HTML file is registered in the Local Repository.

Command Line - INPUT

```
git log
```

Command Line - RESPONSE

```
commit 651e510f668aa841a49793b4fa18d2de74c41f5c (HEAD ->master)
Author: bloovee <bloovee2021@gmail.com>
Date: Sat Oct 28 11:03:27 2023 +0800

    the first commit
```

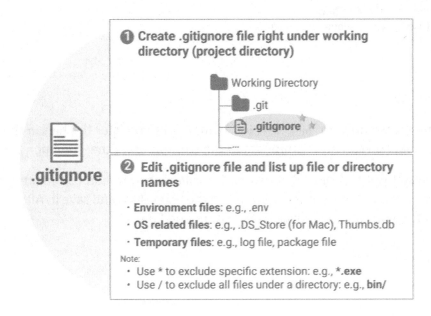

❶ Create .gitignore file right under working directory (project directory)

Working Directory
— .git
— .gitignore

.gitignore

❷ Edit .gitignore file and list up file or directory names

· **Environment files**: e.g., .env
· **OS related files**: e.g., .DS_Store (for Mac), Thumbs.db
· **Temporary files**: e.g., log file, package file

Note:
· Use * to exclude specific extension: e.g., ***.exe**
· Use / to exclude all files under a directory: e.g., **bin/**

Files that you don't want Git to track

One of the key values of Git is sharing files. There are files or directories which you may not want to share or you don't need to share. For example, the *.env* file may contain passwords or other secret information. Suppose you keep the file in your project directory. In that case, Git detects the file and it will be stored in the Remote Repository when you push the project directory into the Remote Repository. If you are a Mac user, you may see a *.DS_Store* file as a hidden file in each directory. This file is used to store custom attributes of the folder on your computer, such as the position of icons or the choice of a background image. This file is also not necessary for a coding project and doesn't require sharing with other developers.

The .gitignore file

To exclude those files from the Git version control system, Git uses the *.gitignore* file. The files and directories written in the .gitignore file are excluded from the Git version control system.

Besides the *.env* file and OS-specific files, log files and package files are also typically written in the *.gitignore* file.

Executing this is very simple. You just need to do the following actions.

1. Create a .gitignore file right under the project directory (the same level as .git directory)

2. In the .gitignore file, list up files or directories you want to exclude from the Git version control system and save the .gitignore file

To understand the concept more clearly, please go through the practice section below.

Practice

Developer A (Project Owner Role)

Objective:
Create a .gitignore file and test it

1. Prepare a test file

Create .env file and run the **git status** command. The **git status** command gives you the status of the files that are recognized by the Git system.

Command Line - INPUT

```
$ touch .env
$ git status
```

You can see that the .env file is recognized by the Git system as shown below. The response says "untracked" but these files are already recognized by the Git version control system. The status tells that those files are not added to the *Staging Area*, which will be explained in more detail later.

Command Line - RESPONSE

```
On branch master
No commits yet
Untracked files:
    (use "git add ..." to include in what will be committed)
        .env
nothing added to commit but untracked files present (use "git add" to track)
```

2. Create and edit the .gitignore file

Create the **.gitignore** file.

Command Line - INPUT

```
touch .gitignore
```

You'll see the **.gitignore** file in the VS Code.

Open the file and edit it by adding *.env*. For Mac OS, also add *.DS_Store*. This file is an auto-generated file by Mac OS to store custom attributes of its containing folder, such as folder view options, icon positions, etc. You don't need to add *.DS_Store* for Windows.

.gitignore

```
1 .env
2 .DS_Store
```

Make sure that you save the file.

3. Check that the selected files are ignored

Run the **git status** command to check the files recognized by the Git system

Command Line - INPUT

```
git status
```

You can see that the *.env file* and *.DS_Store* file are no longer recognized by the Git system as shown below.

```
On branch master
No commits yet
Untracked files:
    (use "git add ..." to include in what will be committed)
        .gitignore
nothing added to commit but untracked files present (use "git add" to track)
```

Delete the *.env file* as it will not be used in the following sections.

(As the *.DS_Store* file is an auto-generated file by Mac OS, you don't need to delete it. Even if you delete it, it will be automatically generated again.)

4. Commit the .gitignore file

As the .gitignore file itself needs to be tracked by Git, add the file to the *Staging Area* and make a commit by running the command below.

Command Line - INPUT

```
$ git add .
$ git commit -m "added .gitignore file"
```

You can confirm that the file has been committed.

Command Line - RESPONSE

```
git commit -m "added .gitignore file"
[master acc4aa4] added .gitignore file
 1 file changed, 2 insertions(+)
 create mode 100644 .gitignore
```

Tips: .gitignore file useful writing rules

Excluding files with a certain extension: if you want to exclude all the files with a specific extension, you can put "*" right before the extension like *exe*.

Excluding files under a certain directory: If you want to exclude all the files under a certain directory, you can put "/" right after the directory name like *bin/*.

117

Tips: gitignore.io

Listing all necessary items for the **.gitignore** file may be time-consuming. You can use **gitignore.io**[5] to check typical files or directories that should be listed in the .gitignore file for a certain type of project.

For example, if you are creating a Django-based app, type '**Django**' and click on the **Create button**.

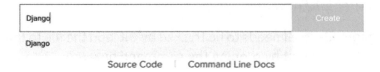

.gitignore.io

Create useful .gitignore files for your project

| Django | Create |

Django

Source Code | Command Line Docs

You'll see a list of files or directories like in the example below. Copy the list and paste it into your .*gitignore* file.

```
# Created by https://www.toptal.com/developers/gitignore/api/django
# Edit at https://www.toptal.com/developers/gitignore?templates=django

### Django ###
*.log
*.pot
*.pyc
__pycache__/
local_settings.py
db.sqlite3
db.sqlite3-journal
media

# If your build process includes running collectstatic, then you probably don't need or want to include staticfiles/
# in your Git repository. Update and uncomment the following line accordingly.
# <django-project-name>/staticfiles/

### Django.Python Stack ###
# Byte-compiled / optimized / DLL files
*.py[cod]
*$py.class
```

---

5 https://www.toptal.com/developers/gitignore/

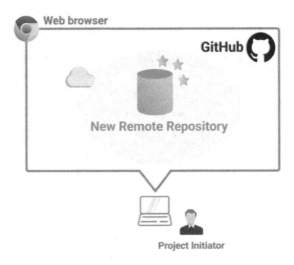

When you want to store and share your project files on GitHub, you need to create a new Remote Repository on GitHub. Creating a Remote Repository and granting access are done through the GitHub web platform. Here are the key steps to create a new Remote Repository.

1. Go to the **GitHub**[6] and sign-in to the account.

2. On the main page, press the green **New** button on the left or click the top right + sign and select **New repository**.

3. On the "**Create a new repository**" page, you need to add a repository name, select public or private, and press the **Create repository** button.

---

6 https://github.com/

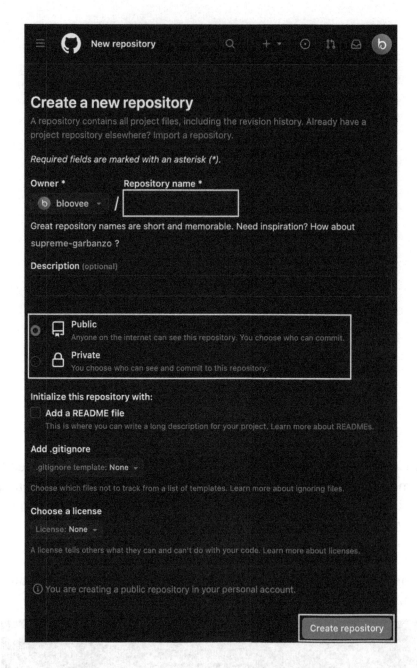

We have an integrated practice section later (**Project Initiator - Grant Remote Repository Access to Project Members**[7]) in this chapter to cover creating a new repository, uploading project documents, and inviting a project member to the repository.

---

7 https://d-libro.com/topic/project-initiator-grant-remote-repository-access-to-project-members?id=practice

Tips: Switch between a private repository and a public repository

You can change the type of repository from public to private or vice versa after creating the repository. Here is an example that shows how to change a private repository to a public repository.

1. Go to the settings page of the repository.

2. Go to the bottom of the page and find **Danger Zone**. Click on the **Change Visibility** button and select **Change to Public**.

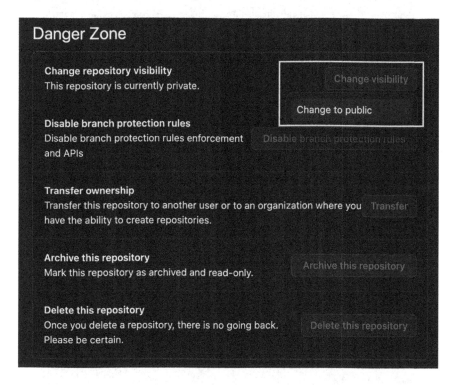

3. There are multiple confirmation messages. Agree with the messages.

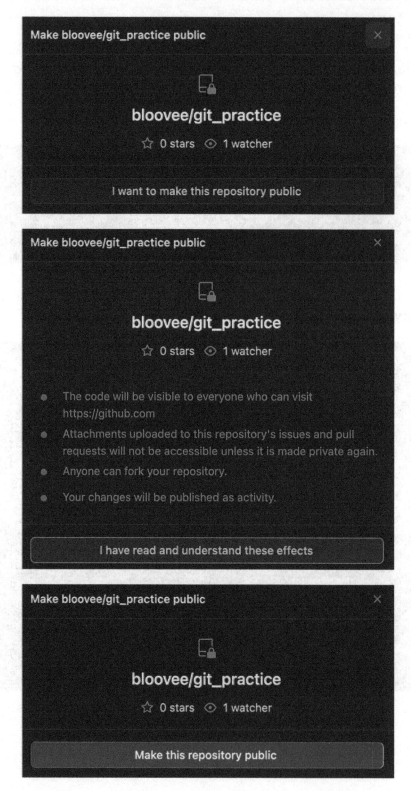

4. You'll see that the repository status has changed from private to public.

Project Initiator – Link Between Remote and Local Repositories (git remote add)

```
$ git remote add origin URL
```

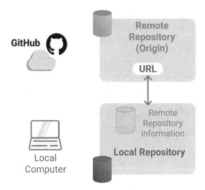

To upload your code from your Local Repository to your Remote Repository, first, you need to connect your Local Repository to your Remote Repository. **git remote add** is the command used to establish the connection.

For the command, you need to specify the URL of your Remote Repository. There are different URLs for different communication protocols. You can choose **HTTPS** or **SSH**.

HTTPS

SSH

The URL structures are like in the examples below. The initial parts of URLs are different. However, the latter parts are the same: GitHub Account Name and Remote Repository Name. **origin** is the default remote Repository name.

1. **HTTPS**: *https://github.com/GitHub Account Name/Remote Repository Name. git*

2. **SSH**: git@github.com:*GitHub Account Name/Remote Repository Name*.git

You can check the Remote Repository URL setting status by running the **git remote -v**.

Project Initiator – Upload Local Repository to Remote Repository (git push)

```
$ git push origin master
```

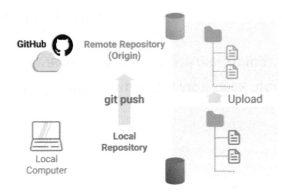

To share your project files through Git Remote Repositories, you need to upload your project directory. **Push** is an action used to upload your project directory or code from your Local Repository to a Remote Repository. **git push** is the command for uploading codes. When you run the command, you need to specify a Remote Repository name and a branch name that you want to upload.

For a simple Git operation, you'll frequently use the **git push origin master** command. **origin** is the default Remote Repository name. **master** is the default branch name. Unless you created another branch, **master** is the only branch in the repository.

Project Initiator – Grant Remote Repository Access to Project Members

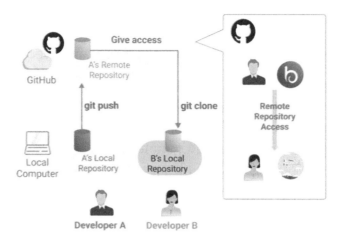

To share the documents, you need to invite your project members to the Remote Repository and give them access to your Remote Repository. This process can be done through the GitHub web platform. Here are the key steps to invite your project members to the Remote Repository.

1. Go to the **Settings** page and select **Manage access**. Press the **Add people** button.

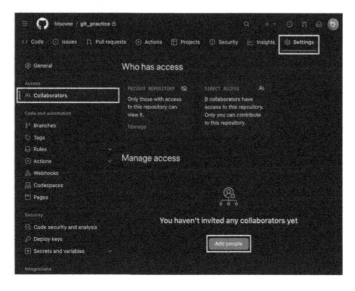

2. You can type the GitHub account or email address of the person who you want to collaborate with. If you input the GitHub account, the website will look up the existing GitHub accounts.

3. When you find the right account, click the **green** button. The account owner will receive an invitation and they can decide either to accept the invitation or to decline the invitation.

In this section, we'll cover a practice section from creating a new repository and uploading project documents, to inviting a project member to the repository.

Here are the four key steps covered in the following practice section.

1. Create a Remote Repository under your GitHub account as the owner.

2. Establish a link between the Local Repository and the Remote Repository by running the **git remote add** command.

3. Upload your code by running the **git push** command.

4. Allow others (collaborators) to access the Remote Repository.

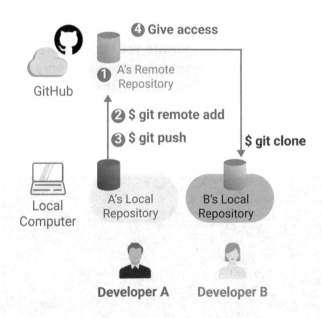

After you complete these four actions, your team member will receive an invitation to access your repository, and he or she will be ready to transfer the code saved in the Remote Repository to their Local Repository.

Practice

Developer A (Project Owner Role)

Objective:
Create a GitHub Remote Repository and be ready to share the project documents with a team member

In this practice, we'll use an example of how *Developer A* (*bloovee*) can share his project directory with *Developer B* (*ocean-blue2022*) via a GitHub Remote Repository.

1. Create a Remote Repository under your GitHub account

Go to the **GitHub**[8] and sign in to the account. On the main page, you can click **+** mark in the navigation top bar and select "**New repository**" or press the green **New** button on the left.

On the "**Create a new repository**" page, you need to add a repository name, select public or private, and press the **Create repository** button. In this demo, we'll use *git_practice* as the repository name (the same as the project directory on the local computer) and make the repository private. There are some options to create additional documents. You can skip them for this practice.

---

8 https://github.com/

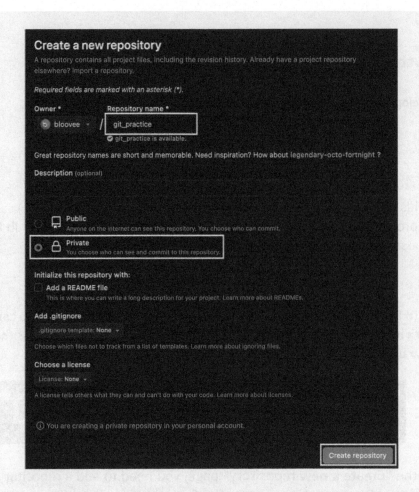

Once you successfully made the new Remote Repository, you can see a page like the one below. Copy the URL for the next action. You can choose HTTPS or SSH depending on which secure communication protocol you want to use.

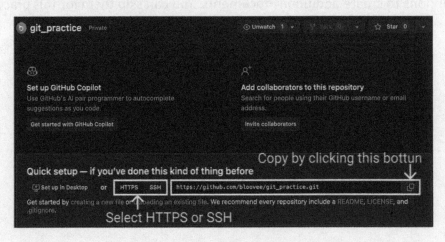

2. Establish a link between the Local Repository and the Remote Repository

Run the following command to establish a link between the Local Repository and the Remote Repository. *origin* is a standard name for the Remote Repository. (When you clone a Remote Repository, the default name of the Remote Repository on your local machine is also *origin*.)

Command Line - INPUT (for HTTPS)

```
git remote add origin https://github.com/bloovee/git_practice.git
```

OR

Command Line - INPUT (for SSH)

```
git remote add origin git@github.com:bloovee/git_practice.git
```

After running the **git remote add** command, there is no command line response. To confirm what you have done, you can check the Remote Repository URL status by running **git remote -v**.

Command Line - INPUT

```
git remote -v
```

For the HTTPS case, you'll see the following response.

Command Line - RESPONSE (for HTTPS)

```
origin https://github.com/bloovee/git_practice.git (fetch)
origin https://github.com/bloovee/git_practice.git (push)
```

Or, for the SSH case, you'll see the following response.

Command Line - RESPONSE (for SSH)

```
origin git@github.com:bloovee/git_practice.git (fetch)
origin git@github.com:bloovee/git_practice.git (push)
```

3. Upload the codes from the Local Repository to the Remote Repository

Run the following command to upload the code from the Local Repository to the Remote Repository. The command line response will be different for HTTPS and SSH.

Command Line - INPUT

```
git push origin master
```

In the HTTPS case, the command line will ask for a username and password to the GitHub account. This password that is asked for is actually not the password of the GitHub account. You need to input the PAT (Personal Access Token) generated before. In the SSH case, the command line may ask for your SSH passphrase if you set it when you generate the SSH key pair. The response example below is the case when we didn't set a passphrase for SSH.

Command Line - RESPONSE

```
Enumerating objects: 6, done.
Counting objects: 100% (6/6), done.
Delta compression using up to 10 threads
Compressing objects: 100% (4/4), done.
Writing objects: 100% (6/6), 601 bytes | 601.00 KiB/s, done.
Total 6 (delta 0), reused 0 (delta 0), pack-reused 0
To github.com:bloovee/git_practice.git
    * [new branch] master -> master
```

To confirm that the code is successfully transferred to the Remote Repository, go to the **GitHub**[9]. You see the project documents are uploaded to the repository.

---

9 https://github.com/

4. Allow Developer B to access to her Remote Repository

Managing GitHub repository will be done on the GitHub GUI. Go to the **Settings** page and select **Manage access**. Press the **Add people** button.

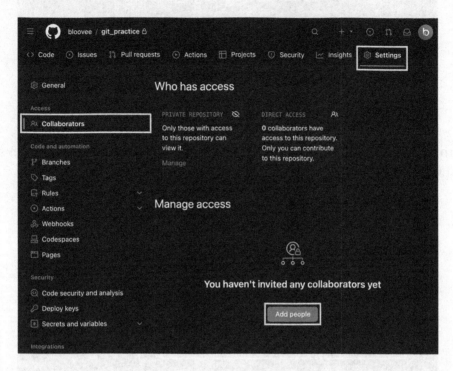

You can type the GitHub account or email address of the person who you want to collaborate with. If you input the GitHub account, the website will look up the existing GitHub accounts as shown below.

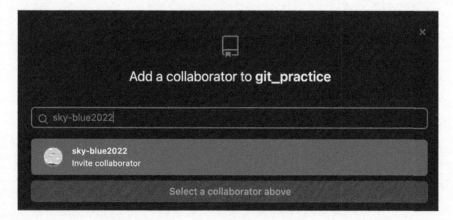

When you find the right account, click the **green** button to send the invitation to the team member.

At this stage, the team member's participation is not confirmed. You can see that GitHub is awaiting the team member's response.

We'll explain how the project member can confirm the invitation and get access to the Remote Repository on the next topic page.

Project Member – Start Project As Collaborator

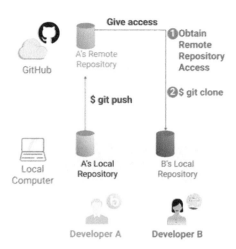

In this page, we'll explain how a project member gains access to the project Remote Repository and starts a project on their local computer.

There are two key steps that you need to do as a project member.

1. **Obtain Remote Repository access** from the owner of the Remote Repository.
   - First, the owner of the Remote Repository needs to invite you to gain access to the Remote Repository.
   - The invitation will be sent to your email. By accepting the invitation, you'll get access to the Remote Repository.

2. Create a copy of the project files in the Remote Repository on your local computer.
   - Once you get access to the Remote Repository, you can transfer the project directory in the Remote Repository to your local computer.
   - To transfer the project directory, run the **git clone** command on your local computer.

— The command also creates a Local Repository that is connected to the Remote Repository so that you can start to interact with the Remote Repository from the command line on your computer.

We have a practice section that covers the steps above on the next topic page.

Project Member – Create Copy of Project Code on Local Computer (git clone)

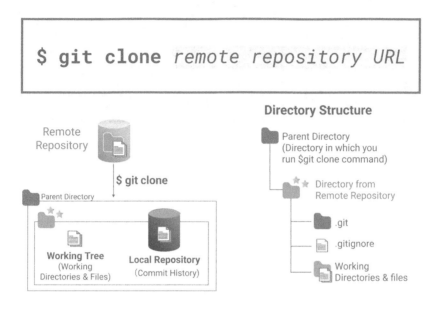

```
$ git clone remote repository URL
```

The **git clone** command is used to create a local copy of a Remote Repository - establish a link with a Remote Repository and bring the project directory from the Remote Repository with commit histories to your local computer.

This command is used only the first time you bring the project directory to your local computer. The **git clone** command establishes a connection between the Rremote Repository and your local computer by registering the URL to define the location of the Remote Repository on your computer. Once the connection is established, you can **Pull** or **Fetch** the Remote Repository.

Pull and Fetch will be explained in Chapter 6.

When you run the **clone** command, you need to specify the URL of the Remote Repository that you want to clone. The URLs for HTTPS and SSH are different. As we explained in Chapter 2, you can choose one of them. You can find the URL of the Remote Repository on the **< > Code** page of the GitHub web platform. You can see the URLs after clicking the green Code button as shown below.

HTTPS **SSH**

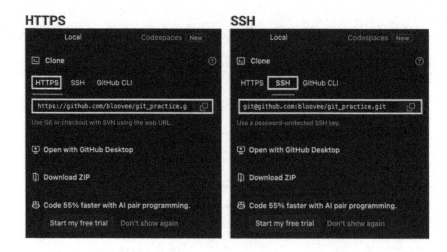

When you clone a Remote Repository, the default name of the Remote Repository on your local computer is *origin*. After you clone a Remote Repository, you can check the Remote Repository name and URL on your computer by running **git remote -v**.

Practice

Developer A (Project Owner Role)

Objective:
Gains access to the project Remote Repository and starts a project as a project member

1. Accept the Remote Repository access invitation

Once the owner of the Remote Repository sends a project member an invitation, the project member will get an email to their registered email address.

In the previous practice, *Developer A* has sent an invitation to *Developer B*. In this practice, we'll explain from the *Developer B*'s point of view. After the invitation is sent out, *Developer B* gets an email like the one below.

GitHub

@bloovee has invited you to collaborate on the
bloovee/git_practice repository

You can accept or decline this invitation. You can also visit @bloovee to learn a bit
more about them.

This invitation will expire in 7 days.

View invitation

Click the **View invitation** button to see the invitation, and accept the invitation
by pressing the **Accept invitation** button.

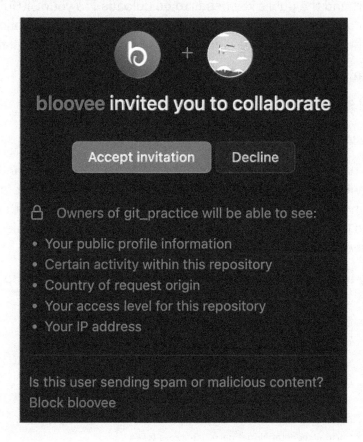

You can access the Remote Repository from your GitHub account as a project member.

2. Prepare for GitHub HTTPS or SSH connection

Before executing the **git clone** command, you need to prepare for GitHub connection with HTTPS or SSH. For HTTPS, you need a PAT. For SSH, you need SSH key pairs and the public key needs to be uploaded to your GitHub platform. If you have not done any of these setups, please check one of the following topic pages. The first one is the easiest and the last one is the most advanced.

- **Generating PAT (Personal Access Token)**[10]
- **GitHub SSH Setup**[11]

3. Set the current working directory

When you run the **git clone** command, the project directory and Git Local Repository will be created under the current working directory. Before running the command, you need to set the current directory carefully to create the repository in the right location. In this practice, we use the main project directory for *Developer B* (e.g., *Dev_B_skyblue*) under the home directory.

A quick way to open the directory with VS Code is using drag & drop.

---

10 https://d-libro.com/topic/generating-pat-personal-access-token
11 https://d-libro.com/topic/github-ssh-setup

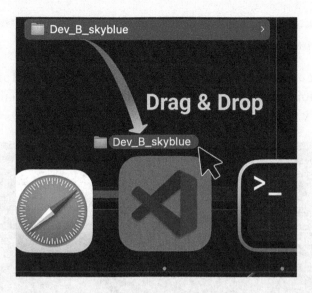

Open a new terminal. You can see that the project's main directory is shown in the *EXPLORER* section on the left and the directory is the current working directory in the terminal.

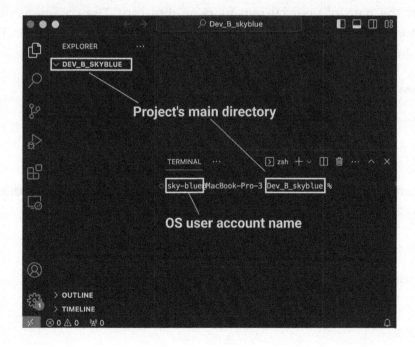

Tips: Changing and check the current working directory in the command line (the cd and pwd command)

When you open a terminal without selecting a specific directory, the current working directory is usually the home directory. ~ (**tilde**) is usually used for the home directory path.

If you are not sure, run the command below. The **cd** command changes your current working directory to the home directory and the **pwd** command returns the path of your current working directory. The commands below are an example. Use your own project directory path when you run the **cd** command.

Command Line - INPUT

```
cd ~/Dev_B_skyblue
pwd
```

After running the commands, you can confirm your current working directory path as shown below.

Command Line - RESPONSE

```
/Users/sky-blue/Dev_B_skyblue
```

4. Clone the repository

To transfer the project directory and repository to your local computer, you need to run the **git clone [Remote Repository URL]** command.

Command Line - INPUT (for HTTPS)

```
git clone https://github.com/bloovee/git_practice.git
```

Or

Command Line - INPUT (for SSH)

```
git clone git@github.com:bloovee/git_practice.git
```

If you have successfully authenticated, you'll see a message like the one below.

Command Line - RESPONSE

```
Cloning into 'git_practice'...
remote: Enumerating objects: 4, done.
remote: Counting objects: 100% (4/4), done.
remote: Compressing objects: 100% (3/3), done.
remote: Total 4 (delta 0), reused 4 (delta 0), pack-reused 0
Receiving objects: 100% (4/4), done.
```

After this, you can see that the *git_practice directory* is generated under the current directory.

Non-Member – Start Project With Replica of Existing Repository (Fork)

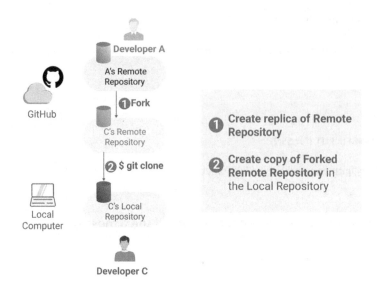

In this page, we'll explain the last case. As GitHub is an open platform, you can access many repositories created by someone else. You may want to leverage an existing repository to start your new coding project.

In this case, you'll create a replica of an existing Remote Repository (but it will be a project independent from the original one). This case is also a rather common approach when you learn from a project that already exists on GitHub public repositories.

There are two key steps for this case.

1. **Create a replica of an existing Remote Repository**. Find a repository that you want to leverage in your project. On the Remote Repository page on GitHub, find the **Fork** button to create a replica and bring it to your GitHub account page.

2. **Clone the Remote Repository**. To start a project, you need to bring the project directories and files under the Remote Repository onto your computer by running the **git clone** command.

Case Example

For this case example, *Developer C* (account: *ocean-blue2022*) will fork the *git_practice* repository owned by *Developer A* (account name: *bloovee*).

1. Create a replica of an existing Remote Repository - Fork

Log in to your GitHub account. In the image below, you can see that *Developer C* signed in to the GitHub platform with the *ocean-blue2022* account.

To go to the repository, search the repository using the search box. In this case, *Developer C* finds the *bloovee/git_practice* public repository.

To **fork** the repository, press the **Fork** button on the top right.

Press the **Create fork** button.

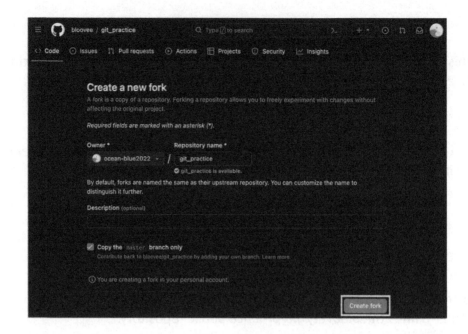

Now, the forked repository *git_practice* is created under the *ocean-blue2022* account

2. Clone the repository to create a local copy on your computer

After you fork the repository on GitHub, the next step is the same as the one we explained in the previous practice. You need to run the **git clone** command to transfer the project directory onto your computer; however, you need to check two things

- **Prepared for GitHub HTTPS or SSH connection**: For HTTPS, you need a PAT. For SSH, you need SSH key pairs and the public key needs to be uploaded to your GitHub platform.

- **Set the current working directory**: Before running the command, you need to decide where you create the project directory and the repository. Change your current working directory using the **cd** command.

Once you have done the above, run the command below.

Command Line - INPUT (for HTTPS)

```
git clone https://github.com/bloovee/git_practice.git
```

Or

Command Line - INPUT (for SSH)

```
git clone git@github.com:bloovee/git_practice.git
```

Command Line - RESPONSE

```
Cloning into 'git_practice'...
remote: Enumerating objects: 3, done.
remote: Counting objects: 100% (3/3), done.
remote: Compressing objects: 100% (2/2), done.
remote: Total 3 (delta 0), reused 3 (delta 0), pack-reused 0
Receiving objects: 100% (3/3), done.
```

After this, the *git_practice* directory will be generated under the directory in which you run the command.

The final status seems the same as the one in the previous practice. However, there is a significant difference between them. In the previous case, you are still collaborating with the owner of the original Remote Repository. In this case, you completely separate the Remote Repository. The forked repository no longer belongs to the original owner of the repository.

Practice

Developer A (Project Owner Role)

Objective:
Learn how to fork a repository and bring it to the local computer

For this practice example, *Developer A* (account name: *bloovee*) will fork the *html-css-introduction* repository owned by *Developer B* (account name: *sky-blue2022*). In your case, you can use any user account as you don't own the *html-css-introduction* repository.

1. Fork the repository

First, go to your GitHub web application and search the repository using the search bar at the top. Type *sky-blue2022/html-css-introduction*.

You'll find the repository. Go to the the repository.

Press the **Fork** button to create a replica of the repository under your GitHub account.

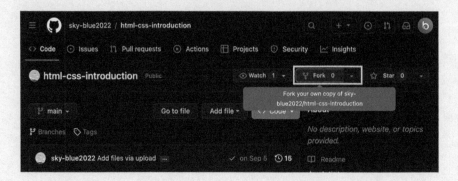

You can change the repository name if you want. Click the **Create fork** button for confirmation.

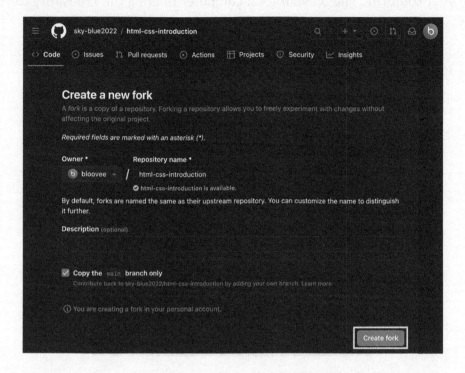

You'll see that a forked repository has been created under your account.

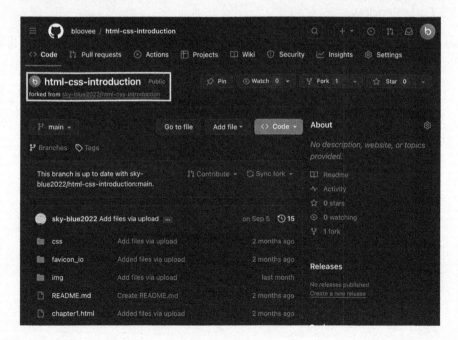

2. Clone the repository

Use your command line on your local computer to bring the repository to your local computer.

Open the project's main directory (e.g., *Dev_A_bloovee*) with VS Code. You can use drag & drop to open the directory.

After opening the project's main directory with VS Code, open a new terminal in the VS Code window.

Make sure that your current working directory in the command line is the project's main directory (e.g., *Dev_A_bloovee*)...

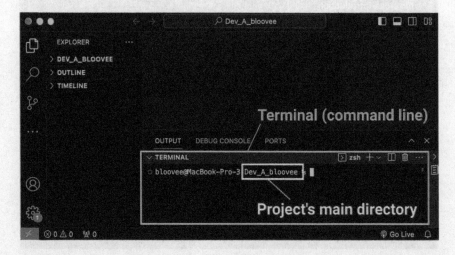

...and run the commands below.

```
git clone https://github.com/sky-blue2022/html-css-introduction.git
```

Or

```
git clone git@github.com:sky-blue2022/html-css-introduction.git
```

```
Cloning into 'html-css-introduction'...
remote: Enumerating objects: 100, done.
remote: Counting objects: 100% (41/41), done.
remote: Compressing objects: 100% (41/41), done.
remote: Total 100 (delta 18), reused 0 (delta 0), pack-reused 59
Receiving objects: 100% (100/100), 21.92 MiB | 4.28 MiB/s, done.
Resolving deltas: 100% (30/30), done.
```

You'll see that the project directory has been transferred into your main project directory.

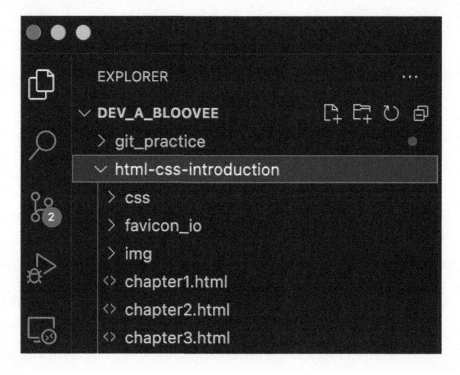

Note: Repository URL

The repository URLs are available under the **Code** section of the repository as shown below. If you want to fork another repository, change the URL to the one for the repository that you want to clone.

Fork vs. Clone

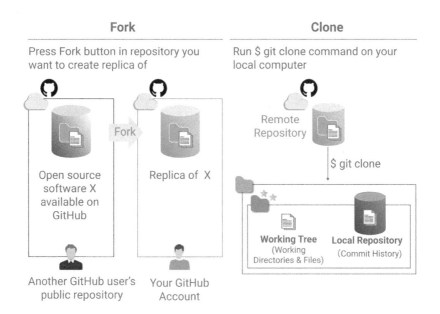

Fork	Clone
Press Fork button in repository you want to create replica of	Run $ git clone command on your local computer

Fork and Clone are often confused with each other. Here we'll give a quick summary of those two concepts.

Fork

Fork is a feature <u>provided by GitHub used to create a replica of a Remote Repository on GitHub</u>. After implementing Fork, the replicated repository will be separated from the original repository. You can modify codes in the replicated repository on your own without permission from the owners of the original repository (within the software license agreement, if any).

Fork is not a git command. It is executed on the GitHub web-based platform. Go to the GitHub site and find the repository which you want to create a replica of. There is a Fork button on the Remote Repository page. Press the Fork button to implement Fork.

Clone

Clone is used to <u>create a local copy of a Remote Repository</u>. To implement Clone, you need to run **git clone** with the Remote Repository name and the URL of the Remote Repository. When the command is executed, the project directory with a Local Repository is created in the current working directory where you run the command. The Local Repository is linked with the Remote Repository so that you can control the interactions between the Local Repository and the Remote Repository through the command line.

Chapter 4
Edit & Commit

Once you launch a project, you can start to write and edit your code. You can save several versions of code in your Local Repository by committing the codes. In this chapter, we'll explain key Git commands used in the cycle of editing and saving code (creating version histories).

The following topics are covered in this chapter.

TOPICS

1. Git Regular Workflow - Edit & Commit
2. Edit and Commit Overview (1)
3. Add Files to Staging Area - git add
4. Commit Files - git commit
5. HEAD and INDEX
6. Check Status of Working Tree and Staging Area - git status
7. Check Commit Histories - git log
8. Check Differences - git diff
9. Restore Files to Working Tree - git restore
10. Undo Changes - git reset
11. Delete Files - git rm
12. Edit and Commit Overview (2)

Git Regular Workflow – Edit & Commit

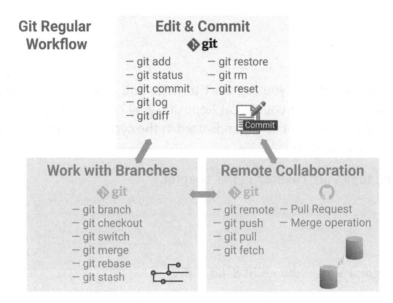

The goal of this chapter is to master the basic cycle of editing and saving code (creating version histories) with key Git commands.

There are 8 key Git commands you will learn in this chapter.

1. **git add**: with this command, you can add files to the *Staging Area* (*INDEX*), where you can prepare and check files to register in your Local Repository.

2. **git status**: with this command, you can check the status of the *Working Tree* (working directory) and the *Staging Area* (*INDEX*). This status lets you see which changes have been staged, which haven't, and which files aren't tracked by Git.

3. **git commit**: with this command, you can register files in your Local Repository. Once the files are registered by this command, you can retrieve the saved version of the set of files anytime.

4. **git log**: with this command, you can check the information of the commit history.

5. **git diff**: with this command, you can check the differences between the *Working Tree*, *Staging Area* (*INDEX*), and *Commits*.

6. **git restore**: with this command, you can <u>bring your *Working Tree* back to the latest commit or a specific commit</u>. This command is useful when you want to clear your edits and go back to a cleaner version.

7. **git rm**: with this command, you can <u>delete files or directories under the *Working Tree* and the *Staging Area* (*INDEX*)</u>. When you want to reflect the deleted status as one of the versions, you need to create another commit.

8. **git reset**: with this command, you can <u>reset the *Staging Area* (*INDEX*) or change commit histories</u> with or without changing the content of your local files.

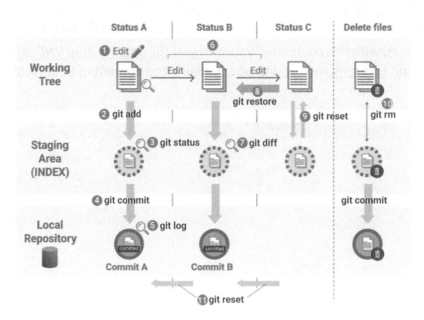

As we already explained in Chapter 1, Git applies the **three-stage architecture**. This architecture allows you to carefully select files and directories to be recorded in the version history. In this page, we'll cover a typical workflow using the three-stage architecture.

Recap of the Git three-stage architecture

Before explaining the typical workflow case example, we'll recap the Git three-stage architecture.

Three-Stage Architecture

- **Working Tree (Working Directory)** is used to edit your working files. The files and directories that you usually see in the project directory are the *Working Tree*.

- **Staging Area** is a buffer area used to prepare your working files for commit. The command to bring the working files into the *Staging Area* is **git add**. You can double-check if the files you added to the *Staging Area* are ready for commit. If the files are ready, you can commit and save them under your Local Repository. The command to commit files is **git commit**.

- **Local Repository** is a place where **committed files** are stored with their version histories. By running the **git commit** command, you can commit your files in the *Staging Area* to save a version under your Local Repository. At this stage, your files are still on your computer and not accessible to others.

A typical workflow of editing and managing commits

To help you understand the three-stage architecture concept more clearly, we'll give you an example of the typical operation cycle - how we manage the three stages using Git commands.

1. Edit code in your project *Working Tree* (e.g., start to create a new app). At this point, the status of the project files is unstaged (or untracked if you create a new file).

2. Once the code is updated, bring the files to the *Staging Area* using the **git add** command.

3. Check the status of the *Working Tree* and the *Staging Area* by running the **git status** command.

4. To save a version of the code, commit the files and record the version in the Local Repository using the **git commit** command.

5. To see the version history, run the **git log** command. You can see the commit history with the commit hash.

6. Then, you can further edit the code to add another feature (under the *Working Tree*) and repeat the above cycle (2 ~ 5).

7. To check the differences in code among the different stages and commits, run the **git diff** command.

8. If you want to reverse your recent edits in the *Working Tree* and bring the latest saved version (latest commit) back to the *Working Tree*, you can run the **git restore** command.

9. If you see errors in the files already in the *Staging Area*, you can clear the files in the *Staging Area* by running the **git reset** command.

10. When you want to delete files or directories from the *Working Tree* or *Staging Area*, you can run the **git rm** command. After running the **git rm** command, you need to run the **git commit** command to reflect the deleted status in the commit histories.

11. **git reset** is also useful when you want to change version history. By specifying a commit hash when you run the command, you can erase the commit history after the specified commit.

Add Files to Staging Area – git add

```
$ git add directory or file path
```

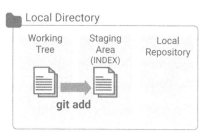

Related commands / options

Add all files under current directory
```
$ git add .
```

Add all changes under Working Tree
```
$ git add -A
```

git add is the command used when you want to add files to the *Staging Area*, where you can prepare and check files for registering in your Local Repository.

Add files or directories with a specific path

When running the command, you need to specify which files or directories to add to the *Staging Area*.

When you want to stage a specific file or directory, you can write the file path or directory path as shown below.

```
git add [directory or file path]
```

Add all files under the current directory

When you want to stage all the files and directories under your current directory, you can use the period ".".

```
git add .
```

Add all changes under the working tree

When you want to stage only the files changed from the latest commit (*HEAD*), you can use the "**-A**" option.

```
git add -A
```

Commit Files – git commit

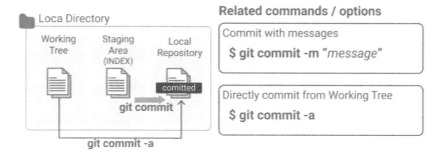

```
$ git commit
```

Loca Directory

| Working Tree | Staging Area (INDEX) | Local Repository |

git commit

comitted

git commit -a

Related commands / options

Commit with messages

$ git commit -m *"message"*

Directly commit from Working Tree

$ git commit -a

git commit is the command to register files in your Local Repository. Once the files are registered with the **git commit** command, you can retrieve the saved version of the set of files anytime.

Commit message

When you commit files, you need to write some messages about the commit. The messages are recorded along with the code. Typically, you describe what changes were made.

When you run the commit command without the "**-m**" option, which will be explained below, the command line will get into the waiting mode...

Command Line

```
$ | git commit
  | hint: Waiting for your editor to close the file...
```

...while the text editor will open up for adding a commit message.

```
<> git_practice.html M ●      ◆ COMMIT_EDITMSG ●

git_practice > .git > ◆ COMMIT_EDITMSG
    1  |
    2     # Please enter the commit message for your changes. Lines starting
    3     # with '#' will be ignored, and an empty message aborts the commit.
    4     #
    5     # On branch master
    6     # Changes to be committed:
    7     # modified:   git_practice.html
    8     #
    9
```

After typing the commit message, save it and close the file.

Text Editor

the first commmit
Please enter the commit message for your changes. Lines starting
with '#' will be ignored, and an empty message aborts the commit.
#
On branch master
Changes to be committed:
modified: git_practice.html
#

A new commit will be created as shown below.

Command Line

$ | git commit
  | [master 0d93dbb] the first commit
  | 1 file changed, 1 insertion(+), 1 deletion(-)

There are some frequently used short-cut options for this command.

"-m" option

The **-m** option is **used to describe a commit message directly in the command.** If you don't use this option, a registered text editor is launched automatically. In that case, you need to write a commit message in the text editor, save it, and close the text editor. The **-m** option is useful to make the operation quicker.

git commit -m "Fixed Bugs"

"-a" option

Another option frequently used is the -a or --all option. To commit a modified or deleted file, you need to add the status to the *Staging Area* by running the **git add** command. The -a or --all option allows you to <u>directly make a commit (skip the Staging Area)</u>. This option is not applicable to untracked files. For example, when you create a new file from the last commit, the file needs to be added to the *Staging Area* by running the **git add** command.

```
git commit -a
```

Combine options

You can use these two options together. For example, if you modify some files to fix a bug and you want to commit the status, you can run the following command.

Command Line
```
git commit -a -m "Fixed Bugs"
```

Or

```
git commit -am "Fixed Bugs"
```

> ### Note: No file path is needed for the git commit command
>
> Another note for the **git commit** command is that you don't need to specify a file or directory path differently from the **git add** command. Because the Git system already tracks the files in the *Working Tree* and *Staging Area*, the **git commit** command automatically detects what files need to be committed.

Tips: Git source control in VS Code

VS Code also provides a GUI (Graphic User Interface) for the Git source control feature. Using the feature, you can make commits using the GUI.

After you edit your code, you can make a commit by typing a commit message and pressing the Commit button.

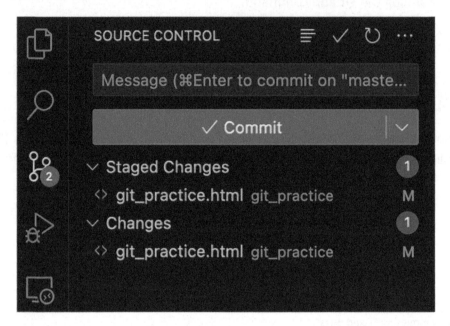

Using the Git source control GUI, you can do many other things. See the following link to learn more about the Git source control in VS Code - **Using Git source control in VS Code**[1].

---

1 https://code.visualstudio.com/docs/sourcecontrol/overview

HEAD and INDEX

HEAD and INDEX

Local Project Directory

Working Tree   Staging Area **(INDEX)**   Local Repository

git add   git commit   Added to version history   **HEAD** (Latest commit)

Commit History

When you start working with Git, you'll see the terms **HEAD** and **INDEX** frequently. Here are the definitions of these terms.

HEAD

The latest commit (the latest version) is called **HEAD**. As you can create many commits during your coding project, having a special name for the latest commit is useful.

The concept of *HEAD* is also useful for understanding the branch workflow which will be explained in Chapter 5.

To indicate one commit before *HEAD*, you can use **HEAD~** (tilde) or **HEAD^** (Caret). The meaning of ~ and ^ will be different in a multi-branch context. It will be explained in the next chapter.

INDEX

INDEX is another term for the staging area as was already explained before. From this page onwards, we use *INDEX* instead of *Staging Area.*

Check Status of Working Tree and Staging Area – git status

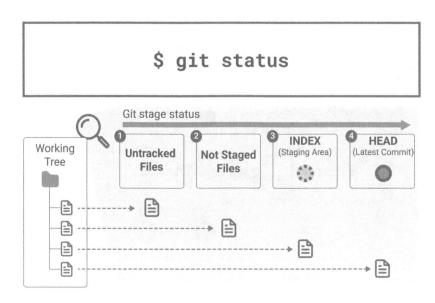

```
$ git status
```

git status is the command that can be used to see the status of the *Working Tree* and the *INDEX*. This status lets you see which changes have been staged, which haven't, and which files aren't tracked by Git.

There are two types of information that the **git status** command provides: **branch status** and **commit status**. In this page, we'll mainly cover the second one (commit status).

Information provided by the git status command

1. Branch status: on which branch you are currently working (the branch concept will be explained in the next chapter)

2. Commit status mainly covers the following status

- Existence of untracked files
- Existence of not staged files
- Files in INDEX (Staging Area) but not committed yet
- All files are tracked and committed

Here are detailed explanations with examples of typical **git status** responses.

1. Existence of untracked files

When you haven't run a commit before and haven't staged any files, the files can have the statuses shown in the illustration below.

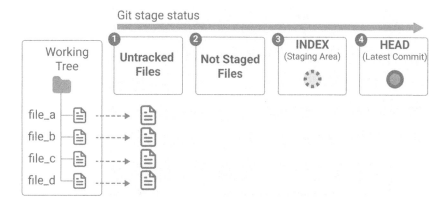

When you run the **git status** command, you'll see a message like below.

git status response

```
On branch master
No commits yet
Untracked files:
    (use "git add <file>..." to include in what will be committed)
        file_a
        file_b
        file_c
        file_d
```

2. Existence of not staged files

In typical git operations, you'll add the files to *INDEX*...

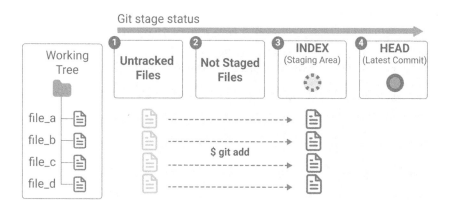

...and commit the files.

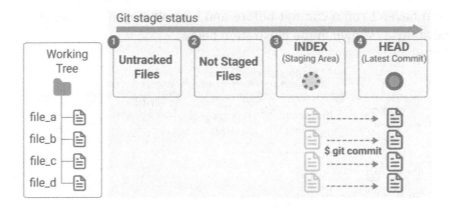

After everything is committed, you may edit some files like in the illustration below. The files are already tracked in the operations above but changes are not staged yet.

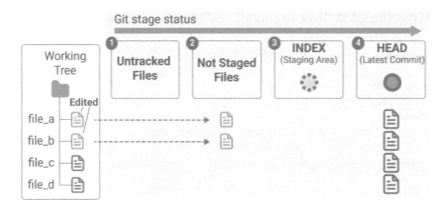

When you run the **git status** command under this situation (before you add the changes to *INDEX*), you'll see a message like below.

git status response

```
On branch master
Changes not staged for commit:
    (use "git add <file>..." to update what will be committed)
    (use "git restore <file>..." to discard changes in working directory)
        modified: file_a
        modified: file_b
```

3. Files in the INDEX (Staging Area) but not committed yet

If you staged the modified files by the **git add** command but have not committed them yet, the files can have the statuses shown in the illustration below.

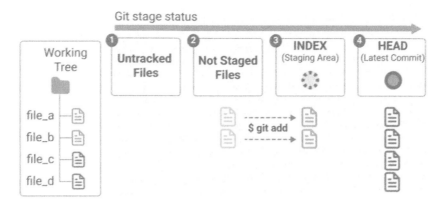

When you run the **git status** command in this situation (before you commit the changes), you'll see a message like below.

git status response

```
On branch master
Changes to be committed:
    (use "git restore --staged <file>…" to unstage)
        modified: file_a
        modified: file_b
```

4. All files are tracked and committed

After you commit all the changes like in the illustration below...

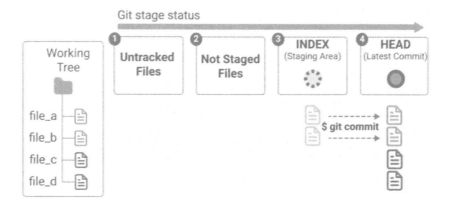

..., you'll see a message like below.

```
On branch master
nothing to commit, working tree clean
```

Check Commit Histories – git log

$ git log

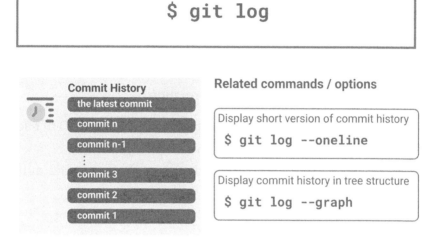

Commit History

- the latest commit
- commit n
- commit n-1
- ⋮
- commit 3
- commit 2
- commit 1

Related commands / options

Display short version of commit history
$ git log --oneline

Display commit history in tree structure
$ git log --graph

git log is the command used when you want to get the commit history information of the repository.

Key information that the git log command provides

For example, when you run this command...

```
git log
```

...you'll see a message like the one below. In this case, you can see that there are two commits.

```
commit acc4aa4c31b033bc39113073ef404e14a970e65b (HEAD -> master, origin/
master)
Author: bloovee <bloovee2021@gmail.com>
Date: Sat Oct 28 11:23:58 2023 +0800

    added .gitignore file

commit 651e510f668aa841a49793b4fa18d2de74c41f5c
Author: bloovee <bloovee2021@gmail.com>
Date: Sat Oct 28 11:03:27 2023 +0800

    the first commit
```

For each commit, there are four lines of information.

1. The first line is commit hash. The commit hash is a unique ID of each commit. When you want to retrieve a commit, you need this hash.
2. The second line is the username and email address of the author of the commit.
3. The third line is the date and time of the commit.
4. The last line is the commit message.

Key options

"--oneline" option

Displays each commit in one line. If commit histories become too long, you may want to skip some items to display. The **--oneline** option is useful for shortening the descriptions. With this option, each commit history is shown with one line.

When you run the command below...

```
git log --oneline
```

You'll see the command line response as shown below.

```
acc4aa4 (HEAD -> master, origin/master) added .gitignore file
651e510 the first commit
```

"--graph" option

Displays commits with a graph. With the **--graph** option, you can see the branch diversion or integration history visually. It is effective when commit histories are more complicated with multiple branches. The branch concept will be explained in the next chapter. The following is an example of running **git log** with the **--graph** and **--oneline** option.

When you run the command below...

```
git log --oneline --graph
```

...and when there are multiple branches, you'll see the commit history in a tree structure.

```
*   b5105dc (HEAD -> master) Merged branch A
|\
| *   8fef9f1 (Branch_A) Merged branch B
| |\
| | * 3ab0477 (Branch_B) Edit 5 on branch B
| |/
| *   e83087e Edit 4 on branch A
| *   8fcc58c Edit 3 on branch A
* |   a815b57 Edit 2 on master branch
* |   931aef2 Edit 1 on master branch
|/
* 5c1fd7a First Commit
```

Tips: Exit from the git log display mode

When you run the **git log** command, the command line switches to a different display mode in which you cannot type. To go back to the original mode, you need to press the **q** key.

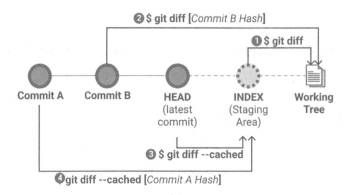

git diff is the command used when you want to know the <u>differences between the Working Tree</u>, <u>the INDEX (Staging Area), and commit histories</u>.

There are four types of differences you can get with the command.

1. **Difference between the Working Tree and INDEX**: When you simply run **git diff**, you'll see this difference.

2. **Difference between the Working Tree and one of the commits**: To see this difference, you need to indicate a commit hash after **git diff**.

3. **Difference between INDEX and HEAD** (the latest commit): The **--cached** option allows you to see the difference between *INDEX* and one of the commit histories. When you don't specify a commit hash, the command gives you the difference between *INDEX* and **HEAD** (the latest commit)

4. **Difference between INDEX and a specific commit**: When you see this difference, you need to specify a commit hash after the **--cached** option.

Practice

Developer A (Project Owner Role)

Objective:
Practice several git commands and test the git diff command

1. Open the practice HTML file

In this practice, we'll use the same practice file that was used in the previous chapter: *git_practice.html*.

The initial file content is shown below. First, confirm that the color status is **blue** which we'll change later.

git_practice.html

```
<!doctype html>
<html lang="en">
<head>
<style>
h1 {
    color: blue;
    font-size:80px
}
</style>
</head>
<body>
<h1>Hello World!</h1>
</body>
```

2. Edit the HTML file and make commits

In the HTML file, change the color property to **green** as shown below. Keep the rest of the code unchanged and save the file.

git_practice.html

```
h1 {
    color: green;
    font-size:80px
}
```

Then, make a new commit.

```
$ git commit -a -m "Modified commit"
```

```
[master 446fa13] Modified commit
 1 file changed, 1 insertion(+), 1 deletion(-)[master 446fa13] Modified commit
 1 file changed, 1 insertion(+), 1 deletion(-)
```

To check the commit status and commit hash, run the **git log** command with the **--oneline** option like below.

```
git log --oneline
```

The command line returns the following commit log with a short version of commit hash.

```
446fa13 (HEAD -> master) Modified commit
acc4aa4 (origin/master) added .gitignore file
651e510 the first commit
```

To create different statuses between the *INDEX* (*Staging Area*) and the latest commit (**HEAD**), further change the color status to yellow.

```
h1 {
    color: yellow;
    font-size:80px
}
```

<u>After saving the file</u>, stage the file by running the following command.

```
git add -A
```

Lastly, change the color status to **red** and <u>save the file</u> to create a different status for the *Working Tree*.

git_practice.html

```
h1 {
    color: red;
    font-size:80px
}
```

By this moment, the status of your *git_practice.html* file's commits, *INDEX*, and the *Working Tree* becomes the following. To simplify the illustration, we skipped the second commit *"added .gitignore file"*, which is not used in this practice anyway.

Prepared settings for this practice

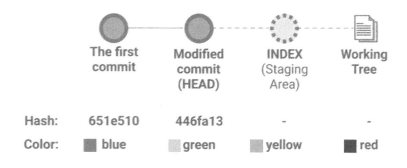

	The first commit	Modified commit (HEAD)	INDEX (Staging Area)	Working Tree
Hash:	651e510	446fa13	-	-
Color:	■ blue	green	yellow	■ red

3. Check for differences

Using the information above, let's confirm the differences in several combinations.

Difference between the Working Tree and INDEX (Case 1)

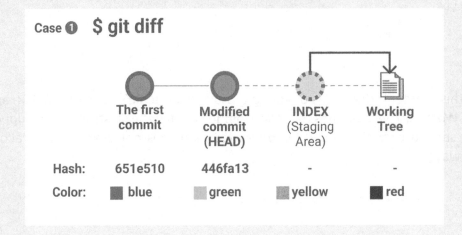

Command Line - INPUT

```
git diff
```

Command Line - RESPONSE

```
diff --git a/git_practice.html b/git_practice.html
index 9520b03..cd27dd6 100644
--- a/git_practice.html
+++ b/git_practice.html
@@ -3,7 +3,7 @@
    <head>
       <style>
       h1 {
          - color: yellow;
          + color: red;
          font-size:80px
       }
       </style>
```

You can see a record showing that the color statuses are the following:

- The older color (*INDEX*) is **yellow**.
- The newer color (*Working Tree*) is **red**.

Difference between the Working Tree and one of the commits (Case 2)

Case ❷ $ git diff HEAD

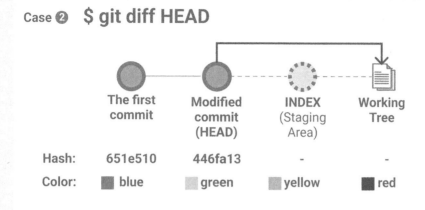

	The first commit	Modified commit (HEAD)	INDEX (Staging Area)	Working Tree
Hash:	651e510	446fa13	-	-
Color:	■ blue	■ green	■ yellow	■ red

To check the difference between the *Working Tree* and **HEAD**, run the command below.

Command Line - INPUT

```
git diff Head
```

Or

```
git diff 446fa13
```

446fa13 is the commit hash of **HEAD**.

Command Line - RESPONSE

```
<style>
    h1 {
        - color: green;
        + color: red;
        font-size:80px
    }
</style>
```

You can see a record showing that the color statuses are the following:

- The older color (**HEAD**) is **green**.
- The newer color (*Working Tree*) is **red**.

Difference between INDEX and HEAD (Case 3)

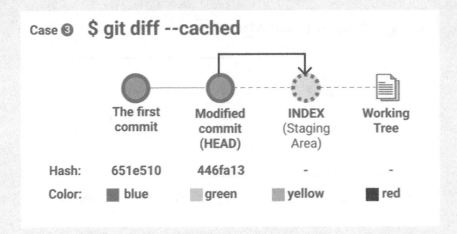

To check the difference between *INDEX* and **HEAD**, run the command below.

Command Line - INPUT

```
git diff --cached
```

Command Line - RESPONSE

```
<style>
    h1 {
        - color: green;
        + color: yellow;
        font-size:80px
    }
</style>
```

You can see a record showing that the color statuses are the following:

- The older color (**HEAD**) is **green**.
- The newer color (*INDEX*) is **yellow**.

You can see a record showing that the color status has changed from **green** to **yellow**.

Difference between INDEX and a specific commit (Case 4)

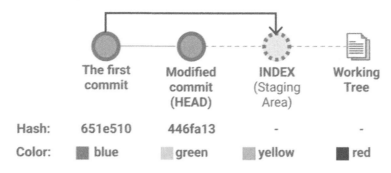

Case ❹ $ git diff --cached [commit hash]

	The first commit	Modified commit (HEAD)	INDEX (Staging Area)	Working Tree
Hash:	651e510	446fa13	-	-
Color:	■ blue	■ green	■ yellow	■ red

To check the difference between *INDEX* and the first commit, run the command below. **651e510** is the commit hash of the first commit.

Command Line - INPUT

```
git diff --cached 651e510
```

Command Line - RESPONSE

```
<style>
    h1 {
        - color: blue;
        + color: yellow;
        font-size:80px
    }
</style>
```

You can see a record showing that the color statuses are the following:

- The older color (commit **651e510**) is **blue**.
- The newer color (*INDEX*) is **yellow**.

Note: Check differences between branches

The **git diff** command can be used for checking differences between branches. If you want to see the differences between *Branch_1* and *Branch_2*, run the following command.

Command Line - INPUT

```
git diff [Branch_1]..[Branch_2]
```

The differences are shown after + or -. + means that the lines of code were added in *Branch_2* compared to *Branch_1*. - means that the lines of code were deleted in *Branch_2* compared to *Branch_1*.

Command Line - RESPONSE

```
+ code added
- code deleted
```

Branch operations will be explained in more detail in Chapter 5.

```
$ git restore directory or file path
```

Commit
History

Staging
Area

Related commands / options

Restore file from specific commit or Head
```
$ git restore [file path] -s [commit hash]
```
or
```
$ git restore [file path] -s Head
```

The following command gives the same results
```
$ git checkout - [directory or file path]
```

git restore is the command used if you want to bring your *Working Tree* back to the latest commit or a specific commit. This command is useful when you want to clear your edits and go back to a cleaner version. There are typically two approaches to using this command. One is without any option and the other is with the -s option. By using the -s option, you can specify a commit that you want to retrieve.

1. No option

When running the following command, you'll see two different results depending on the status of the *INDEX* (*Staging Area*).

```
git restore [ file path or directory path ]
```

When a staged file exists:

The *Working Tree* goes back to the same status as the *INDEX* (*Staging Area*)

When there is no staged file:

The *Working Tree* goes back to the same status as the latest commit (*HEAD*)

Note: git checkout [directory or file path] also gives the same results as this command.

2. "-s" option: restore files or directories from a specific commit

You can restore files or directories from a specific commit by running the following command.

```
git restore [file path or directory path] -s [Commit Hash]
```

You can use *HEAD* instead of a *commit hash* if you want to go back to the latest commit version.

> ## Tips: Run the git command for the current working directory
>
> If you use **period** "." as a directory path, all the files and directories under the current directory will be restored. For example, if you want to restore all the files under the current working directory using commit **1234567**, run the command below.
>
> ```
> git restore . -s 1234567
> ```

Practice

Developer A (Project Owner Role)

Objective:
Practice the git restore command with different scenarios

1. Practice file preparation

In this practice, we'll use the same example as in the **git diff** practice explained earlier. Please review the practice section of the **git diff** page if you haven't gone through it yet. The practice file named *git_practice.html* has the commit history, *INDEX*, and the *Working Tree* illustrated below.

Default settings for this practice

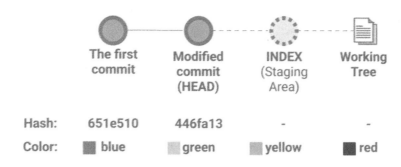

	The first commit	Modified commit (HEAD)	INDEX (Staging Area)	Working Tree
Hash:	651e510	446fa13	-	-
Color:	■ blue	■ green	■ yellow	■ red

When you execute these steps on your computer, you see different *commit hashes*. For your practice, use the *commit hash* generated on your computer.

2. Restore files from different versions

There are three types of approaches to restoring files. The following diagram illustrates which file version you can restore.

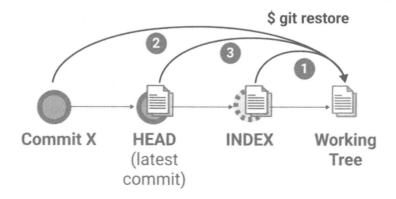

Restore a file from INDEX (1)

By running the following command, you can bring the file status back to the status in the *INDEX*.

```
git restore git_practice.html
```

Check the file. You can see the color status has changed to **yellow**.

git_practice.html

```
h1 {
    color: yellow;
    font-size:80px
}
```

This means that the file is back to the version in the *INDEX*. When you run the **git diff** command, there is no response as the file status in the *INDEX* and *Working Tree* become the same.

If there is no version of the file in the *INDEX*, the **git restore** command brings back the latest commit (*HEAD*). We'll test it later.

Restore a file from a specific commit (2)

By running the following command, you can bring the file status to the same as "The first commit" status.

Command Line - INPUT

```
git restore git_practice.html -s 651e510
```

Check the file. You can see that the color status has changed from **yellow** to **blue**.

git_practice.html

```
h1 {
    color: blue;
    font-size:80px
}
```

This means that the file is back to "The first commit" version.

Restore a file from HEAD (3)

If you want to retrieve the latest commit, you can use *HEAD* instead of the *commit hash* like below.

```
git restore git_practice.html -s HEAD
```

After running the command, you can see that the color changed to **green**.

git_practice.html

```
h1 {
    color: green;
    font-size:80px
}
```

For the next practice exercise, reverse the *INDEX* and the *Working Tree* to the original setting with the following steps.

- Update the color status in the *Working Tree* to **yellow** and save the file.
- Run git add git_practice.html.
- Update the color status in the *Working Tree* to **red** and save the file.

The status should be back to the original settings as shown below.

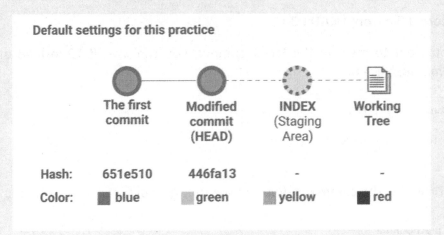

Default settings for this practice

	The first commit	Modified commit (HEAD)	INDEX (Staging Area)	Working Tree
Hash:	651e510	446fa13	-	-
Color:	■ blue	■ green	■ yellow	■ red

Undo Changes – git reset

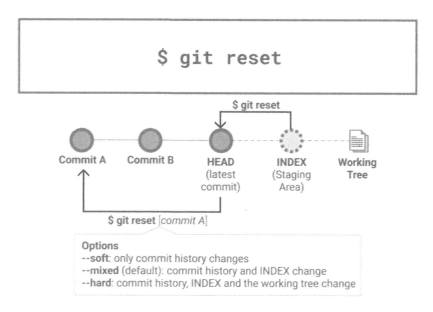

Options
--soft: only commit history changes
--mixed (default): commit history and INDEX change
--hard: commit history, INDEX and the working tree change

git reset is the command used when you want to reset *INDEX* or change commit histories with or without changing the files in the *Working Tree*.

There are mainly two ways you can use this command. We'll explain them using the illustration below. The illustration describes the original status of commits, *INDEX*, and the *Working Tree* before running the **git reset** command.

Original status

	Commit A	Commit B	HEAD	INDEX	Working Tree
file_a					
file_b					
file_c					
file_d					

Original code   Modified code

No commit hash and option

Clear files in INDEX (Staging Area). To clear files in *INDEX*, you need to simply run the **git reset** command like the one below. For this purpose, there is no need to use any option and *commit hash*.

git reset

git reset (no commit hash and option)

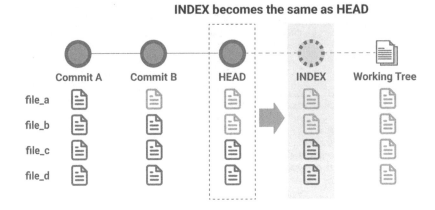

With a commit hash and option (soft, mixed, hard)

To change the commit history, you need to specify which commit to go back to by using a *commit hash*. With this command, the commits made after the *commit hash* will be erased from the history. As the command can create a significant change, you need to carefully run the command.

When changing commit histories, there are three options depending on how you want to change the status of *INDEX* and the *Working Tree*.

"--soft" option

With this option, *INDEX* and *Working Tree* stay unchanged. Only commit histories are reversed as described in the illustration below.

git reset --soft [*commit A hash*]

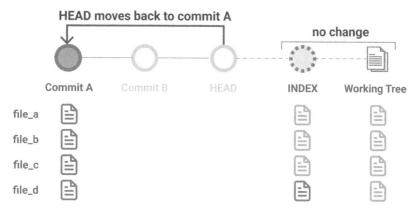

If you want to move back to commit hash **1234567** with this option, run the command below.

```
git reset --soft 1234567
```

"--mixed" option (default)

With this option, only the *INDEX* status will be back to the same status as the commit you designated for this command, as described in the illustration below. The *Working Tree* stays the same. As **--mixed** is the default option, if you don't add an option when running the command, the command will act like with the **--mixed** option.

git reset --mixed [*commit A hash*]

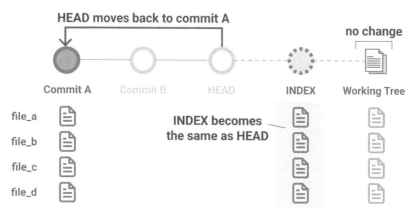

If you want to move back to commit hash **1234567** with this option, run the command below.

```
git reset --mixed 1234567
```

"--hard" option (default)

With this option, the statuses of *INDEX* and the *Working Tree* will be back to the same status as the commit you specified for this command as described in the illustration below. You need to be extremely careful to run the command with this option as all the changes made after the specified commit will be completely erased from the three areas (all commits, *INDEX*, and the *Working Tree*).

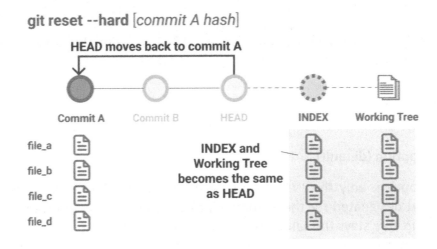

If you want to move back to commit hash **1234567** with this option, run the command below.

```
git reset --hard 1234567
```

Practice

Developer A (Project Owner Role)

Objective:
Practice the git reset command with different options

1. Practice preparation

In this practice, we'll use the same example as in the **git diff** practice explained earlier. Please review the practice section of the **git diff** page if you haven't gone through it yet. The practice file named *git_practice.html* has the commit history, *INDEX*, and the *Working Tree* illustrated below.

Default settings for this practice

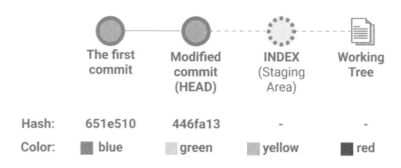

	The first commit	Modified commit (HEAD)	INDEX (Staging Area)	Working Tree
Hash:	651e510	446fa13	-	-
Color:	■ blue	■ green	■ yellow	■ red

When you execute these steps on your computer, you see different **commit hashes**. For your practice, use the **commit hash** generated on your computer.

2. git reset (clear INDEX)

Before running the **git reset** command, check the current status of *INDEX* by running the **git diff** command.

Command Line - INPUT

```
git diff
```

You'll see that the color status of the *Working Tree* is **red** while the color status of *INDEX* is **yellow**. (**git diff** shows the changes in the *Working Tree* compared to *INDEX*:

- After **+** shows the status of the *Working Tree*
- After **-** shows the status of *INDEX*

Command Line - RESPONSE

```
- color: yellow;
+ color: red;
```

To clear the files in *INDEX* you can simply run the **git reset** command. To check the changed status, run the **git diff** command.

Command Line - INPUT

```
git reset
git diff
```

You can see that the color status in *INDEX* is now **green**, which is the same as the *HEAD*.

Command Line - RESPONSE

```
- color: green;
+ color: red;
```

For the next exercise, reverse *INDEX* and the *Working Tree* to the original setting with the following steps.

- Update the color status in the *Working Tree* to **yellow** and save the file.
- Run **git add git_practice.html**.
- Update the color status in the *Working Tree* to **red** and save the file.

To confirm the status is back to the original, run the **git diff** command.

Command Line - INPUT

```
git diff
```

If you see that the color status is the ones below, the color of *INDEX* is back to **yellow**, and the *Working Tree*'s color is **red**.

```
- color: yellow;
+ color: red;
```

Once you confirm that the status is back to the same as the practice default settings, go to the next exercise.

3. git reset --soft

git reset with the **--soft** option is used to change only commit histories. In this practice, we'll target going back to *"The first commit"*, whose *commit hash* is **651e510**. On your computer, you see a different hash. <u>You need to use the **_commit hash_** generated on your computer.</u>

To execute the command and confirm the results, run the **git reset --soft** command followed by **git log**.

```
git reset --soft 651e510
git log --oneline
```

In the command line response, you see that *"Modified commit"* disappears and *HEAD* becomes" *The first commit"* (**651e510**) like below.

```
651e510 (HEAD -> master) The first commit
```

Also, check the status of *INDEX* and the *Working Tree* by running the **git diff** command.

```
git diff
```

You'll see that *INDEX* and the *Working Tree* remain the same.

- *INDEX* -> **yellow** (after the - mark)
- *Working Tree* -> **red** (after the + mark)

Command Line - RESPONSE

```
- color: yellow;
+ color: red;
```

For the next exercise, reverse the commit history to the original status. When reversing the **git reset** operation, you can use **ORIG_HEAD**.

Tips: ORIG_HEAD

ORIG_HEAD is the commit before the **git reset** command is executed. This is useful for reversing the operation you made using the **git reset** command.

Run the following commands and see that the commit history is back to its original state.

Command Line - INPUT

```
git reset ORIG_HEAD
git log --oneline
```

Command Line - RESPONSE

```
446fa13 (HEAD -> master) Modified commit
acc4aa4 (origin/master) added .gitignore file
651e510 the first commit
```

4. git reset --mixed

The **--mixed** option is the default setting. You can run the command without the option to get the same results. You can try the command both with the option and without the option. You need to use the ***commit hash*** generated on your computer.

```
git reset --mixed 651e510
```

Or

```
git reset 651e510
```

To check the results, run the **git log** and **git diff** commands.

Command Line - INPUT

```
git log --oneline
```

Command Line - RESPONSE

```
651e510 (HEAD -> master) the first commit
```

You can see that the *HEAD* is now The first commit (**651e510**)

Command Line - INPUT

```
git diff
```

Command Line - RESPONSE

```
- color: blue;
+ color: red;
```

You can see that *INDEX* becomes the same as the *HEAD* while the *Working Tree* remains the same.

- *INDEX* -> **blue** (after the - mark). This is the same as the *HEAD*.
- *Working Tree* -> **red** (after the + mark)

For the next exercise, do the following.

1. Reverse the commit histories to the original status by running the **git reset ORIG_HEAD** command.

2. Reverse the *INDEX* status with the following steps.
   ° Update the color status in the *Working Tree* to **yellow** and save the file.
   ° Run git add git_practice.html and save the file.
   ° Update the color status in the *Working Tree* to **red** and save the file.

Once you confirm that the status is back to the same as the practice default settings, go to the next exercise.

5. git reset --hard

The **--hard** option is the strongest option. The command will clear the current *Working Tree* and *INDEX* status, and make them the same as the target commit status. As your changes can be completely erased by this command, you need to be very careful when you are running the command with this option.

By running the following commands, you can see the same results as in the case of the other options. You need to use the *commit hash* generated on your computer.

Command Line - INPUT

```
git reset --hard 651e510
git log --oneline
```

Command Line - RESPONSE

```
651e510 (HEAD -> master) the first commit
```

To check the status of *INDEX*, run the **git diff** or **git diff --cached** command. For both commands, you don't get any response as *HEAD*, *INDEX*, and the *Working Tree* reach the same status after the **git reset --hard** command.

To check the difference between *INDEX* and the *Working Tree*, run the command below. There will be no response.

```
git diff
```

To check the difference between *INDEX* and *HEAD*, run the command below. There will be no response.

Command Line - INPUT

```
git diff --cached
```

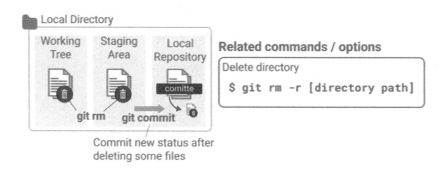

The **git rm** command can delete a file in the *Working Tree* and register the status in *INDEX* (*Staging Area*). To reflect it in the commit history, you need to run the **git commit** command afterward.

The typical command flow is as follows.

1. To delete a file (No option)

When you delete a file, you don't need to add an option.

```
git rm [ file path ]
git commit
```

2. To delete a directory (with the "-r" option)

If you want to delete a directory, you need to use the -r option before the directory path.

```
git rm -r [ directory path ]
git commit
```

Practice

Developer A (Project Owner Role)

Objective:
Check how the git rm command works

1. Prepare a file to delete

For this practice purpose, create a copy of the *git_practice.html* file and commit the new file. Run the **cp** command and commit the file as shown below.

Command Line - INPUT

```
cp git_practice.html git_practice_copy.html
git add .
git commit -m "Added a new file"
```

2. Delete the file

To delete the file run the **git rm** command and check the status with the **git status** command.

Command Line - INPUT

```
git rm git_practice_copy.html
git status
```

After running the command above, you can see the following response

```
On branch master
Changes to be committed:
    (use "git restore --staged <file>..." to unstage)
        deleted:    git_practice_copy.html
```

To register the status in the Local Repository, run the **git commit** command. And check the latest commit log.

```
git commit -m "Deleted the new file"
git log --oneline
```

You can confirm that the deleted status is already registered in the commit histories as shown below.

```
[master a2db148] Deleted the new file
 1 file changed, 13 deletions(-)
 delete mode 100644 git_practice_copy.html
a2db148 (HEAD -> master) Deleted the new file
ad09fe6 Added a new file
651e510 the first commit
```

The demo code is available in this repository (**Demo Code**[1]).

---

1 https://github.com/git-github-introduction/git_practice

Edit and Commit Overview (2)

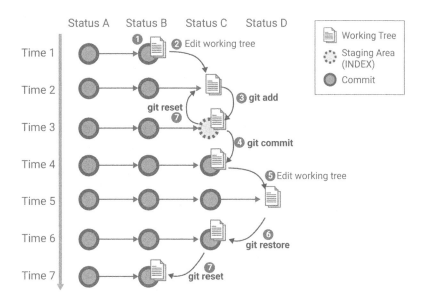

To prepare for the next chapter, we introduce another diagram to explain the edit and commit workflow. This illustration will help you understand how Git works with branches, which will be the focus of the next chapter. The following is the explanation of key icons.

- **Working Tree** or **Working Directory**, which you see on your local computer for daily editing.

- **INDEX** or **Staging Area**. If the *Working Tree* is inside this dotted circle, the edit status of the working tree and the staging area are the same.

- **Commit**. If the *Working Tree* is inside this bold circle, the edit status of the *Working Tree* and the commit are the same.

In this diagram, you can see the progress of coding horizontally. If icons are on the same status column (e.g., *Status B*), the files or directories are in the same status too.

The steps below are the explanation of the diagram in the main figure.

1. First, the *Working Tree* and the latest commit are <u>under the same status (*Status B* in the diagram)</u>.

2. When you edit files under the *Working Tree*, <u>the *Working Tree* status changes from *Status B* to *Status C*</u>.

3. By running the **git add** command, edited files in the *Working Tree* will be registered in the staging area(*INDEX*). At this point, <u>both the *Working Tree* and the staging area are in *Status C*</u>.

4. To make a record of one version using the staged files, run the **git commit** command. <u>The latest commit (*HEAD*) and the *Working Tree* become the same status (*Status C*)</u>.

5. After the commit action, you can continue to edit and <u>move the *Working Tree* forward to *Status D*</u>.

6. However, you may find an error in the committed files. If that is the case, you can restore the files from the latest commit by running the **git restore** command (<u>the *Working Tree* will be back to *Status C*</u>).

7. If you find another error in a committed file, you can also reverse the committed history by running the **git reset --hard** command. For this purpose, you need to set a *commit hash* to specify which commit you want to retrieve.

   — The git reset command can used for clearing the staging area

   — Using different options (**--soft** or **--mixed**), you can keep the *Working Tree* and/or the *INDEX* status.

Chapter 5
Work With Branches

When you add some features while continuing to work on the main code development, you may want to manage several versions of the code. The branch functionality allows you or your team members to work on different versions of code simultaneously. In this chapter, we'll explain branches and related key Git commands. Topics covered in this chapter are the following.

TOPICS

1. Git Regular Workflow - Work With Branches
2. What Is Branch?
3. Branch Operation Basic Life Cycle
4. Create Branch and Check Branch Status - Git Branch
5. Switch Current Branch (1) - Git Checkout
6. Switch Current Branch (2) - Git Switch
7. Merge Branches - Git Merge
8. Fast-Forward Merge
9. Non-Fast-Forward Merge (No Option)
10. Non-Fast-Forward Merge (--no-ff Option)
11. Squash Merge
12. Rebase Branch - Git Rebase
13. Managing Conflict
14. Stash Changes - Git Stash

Git Regular Workflow – Work With Branches

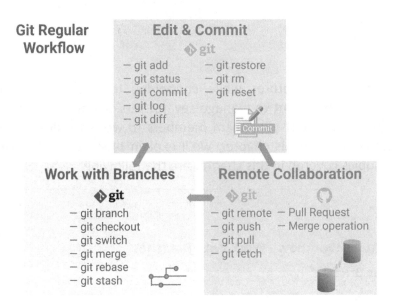

The goal of this section is to help you understand how to manage branches, which is one of the most critical concepts of Git operations.

In this section, we'll cover six key git commands.

- **git branch**: this command is a multi-use command. For example, it is used for creating a new branch, checking branch status, and deleting an unused branch.

- **git checkout**: with this command, you can switch your current branch to a selected branch.

- **git switch**: with this command, you can get the same result as with **git checkout**. It is a newly introduced command used as a substitute for the **git checkout** command.

- **git merge**: with this command, you can merge branches. The merge operation can be done through a Remote Repository on the GitHub website. The merge operation on GitHub will be explained in the next chapter.

- **git rebase**: with this command, you can reapply commits on top of another base branch. This command is useful when you want to streamline the commits diverged into multiple branches. The rebase operation can also be done through a Remote Repository on the GitHub website. This is an option of the merge feature of GitHub.

- **git stash**: with this command, you can separately manage WIP (Work In Progress) codes. When you want to switch the current branch in the middle of editing the *Working Tree*, the edits may prevent you from switching the current branch. In that case, this command is useful. The stashed lines of code are parked somewhere temporarily.

What Is Branch?

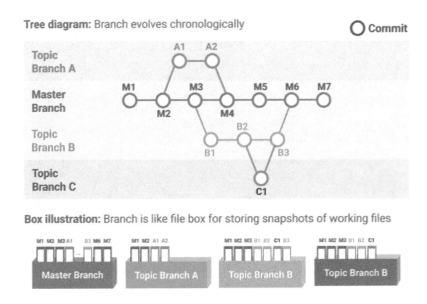

Tree diagram: Branch evolves chronologically ⚪ Commit

Box illustration: Branch is like file box for storing snapshots of working files

Recap of the branch concept

As explained in Chapter 1, a **branch** in Git is an independent line of development with a commit history. Each branch provides a dedicated recording space and has its own coding history (a line of commits).

Branches allow us to manage different versions of the same set of project files simultaneously. For example, one developer can work on adding a new promotion campaign feature while another developer is working on adding a new payment feature to the same web application.

Git provides a **master branch** as a default. (If the repository was initiated on the GitHub platform, the default branch may be called the main branch. Check **master branch vs. main branch**[1].) Unless you create a new branch, all your work is done on the *master* branch. The branch to create a new feature is typically called a **topic branch**.

Once development is completed in a topic branch, you can **merge** it with the *master* branch or its parent branch.

---

1 https://d-libro.com/topic/collaborating-on-git-git-hub-branch?id=main-branch

With the branching functionality, you can efficiently collaborate with others. Or you can even utilize branches by yourself to manage versions to develop different features simultaneously.

Branch illustrations

In this chapter, we'll show how branches are recorded. The main figure shows two illustrations. Both illustrations have codes like *M1*, *M2*, etc. Each of them is a representation of one commit.

- **Tree diagram**: The tree diagram is used to describe how branches diverge and integrate along coding work. This tree diagram is commonly used to get an overview of branches with a commit history.

- **Box illustration**: The box illustration describes how branches store commits. A branch is like a file box for storing snapshots of coding history files. When a new commit is made, a snapshot of the project files for the commit is stored in the file box. Also, when one branch merges with another branch, the history of commits can be carried forward.

Branch tree diagram in the command line

You can confirm the branch tree status in the command line by running the **git log** command with the **--oneline** and **--graph** option.

Command Line - INPUT

```
git log --oneline --graph
```

The command line responses below are examples of the branch logs aligned with the illustrations. The seven-digit code in yellow is a **commit hash** (short version) and you can also see the status of each branch. You can compare the commit messages (*M1, M2,..*) with the illustration. As all branches are merged with the *master* branch, you can see all the branch statuses from the *master* branch. However, for *Branch A, B,* and *C*, you can see the commit histories which are related to their own histories.

Example 1: Master Branch's Commit History

You can see the histories of all the branches from the *master* branch as all the branches are already merged with the *master* branch.

```
*   98a7a09 (HEAD -> master, origin/master, origin/HEAD) M7
*   f44a7b1 M6
|\
| *     55e0a1a (origin/Branch_B, Branch_B) B3
| |\
| | *   089bade (origin/Branch_C,Branch_C) C1
| |/
| * 3d7f400 B2
| * 42ba160 B1
* | c6835c2 M5
* |   fd694e3 M4
|\\
| |/
|/|
| * 59ca1dc (origin/Branch_A, Branch_A) A2
| * cb28ee8 A1
* | 43ca3d2 M3
|/
* 5eb04c5 M2
* eadeda0 M1
```

Example 2: Branch A's Commit History

On the other hand, you have a limited view from *Branch A*. This is because all the changes after commit *A2* were made on the other branches.

```
* 59ca1dc (HEAD, origin/Branch_A, Branch_A) A2
* cb28ee8 A1
* 5eb04c5 M2
* eadeda0 M1
```

Example 3: Branch B's Commit History

You can see that *Branch C* diverged from *Branch B* at commit *B2* and merged with *Branch B* at commit *B3*.

```
* 55e0a1a (HEAD, origin/Branch_B, Branch_B) B3
|\
| * 089bade (origin/Branch_C, Branch_C) C1
|/
* 3d7f400 B2
* 42ba160 B1
* 43ca3d2 M3
* 5eb04c5 M2
* eadeda0 M1
```

Example 4: Branch C's Commit History

You can see that *Branch C* diverged from *Branch B*. However, the commit merging *Branch C* into *Branch B* is not visible from *Branch C*'s status as the merge operation was done on *Branch B*. There is no impact on *Branch C* from the merge operation on *Branch B*.

```
* 089bade (HEAD, origin/Branch_C, Branch_C) C1
* 3d7f400 B2
* 42ba160 B1
* 43ca3d2 M3
* 5eb04c5 M2
* eadeda0 M1
```

The video below shows how different versions of code are displayed when you switch branches.

Open the **Video**[2] in a browser.

---

2 https://static.d-libro.com/01-course-content-images/2041-10-Git-GitHub-Introduction/021-video-insert/
  how-branches-work-in-vs-codeid204110050210-video1.mp4

On the following topic pages, we'll explain how to manage branches in detail.

The demo code is available in this repository (**Demo Code**[3]).

> ## Note: Bring the demo code to your local computer
>
> We'll explain how to run branch-related commands. Here are the heads-up in case you want to try them first.
>
> You can clone the master branch and check the branch status by running the following commands.
>
> **Command Line - INPUT**
>
> ```
> git clone git@github.com:git-github-introduction/what-is-branch-demo.git
> cd what-is-branch-demo
> git branch -a
> ```
>
> Then, check out all other branches.
>
> **Command Line - INPUT**
>
> ```
> git checkout Branch_A
> git checkout Branch_B
> git checkout Branch_C
> git checkout master
> git branch -a
> ```
>
> You'll see that the four remote branches are now available on your local computer. We'll explain the branch concepts and commands in detail in this chapter.

---

3 https://github.com/git-github-introduction/what-is-branch-demo

Branch Operation Basic Life Cycle

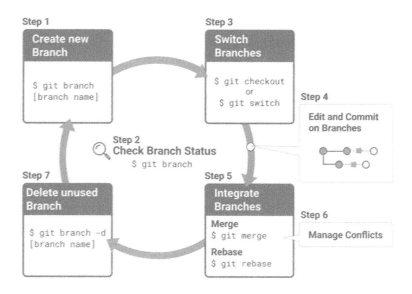

In this page, we'll explain a basic life cycle for the branch operation in seven steps.

Step 1: Create a new branch

As a default setting, you are working on the *master* branch. Edit and commit operations explained in the previous chapter were conducted on the *master* branch.

When you want to separate your work from the *master* branch, you need to create a new branch by running the **git branch [new branch name]** command.

Step 2: Check the branch status

To check your branch status (i.e., the list of branches and the current branch) in the command line, you need to run the **git branch** command. When you specify a branch name, the command creates a new branch. For checking status purposes, you simply run the command without any parameter.

215

Step 3: Switch branches

When you create a new branch by running the **git branch [new branch name]** command, you are still on the original branch; if you are creating a new branch for the first time, you are still on the *master* branch. To move to the new branch, you have to run one of the following commands

- **git checkout [branch name]**
- **git switch [branch name]**

Previously, the **git checkout** command was used only as an option to do this, however, **git switch** command was introduced as a substitute for **git checkout** command. Currently, you can use both commands to get the same result.

Step 4: Edit and Commit on branches

We already explained edit and commit operations in the previous chapter. The edit and commit operations can be applied regardless of the branch you are working on. What you may need to be careful of is on which branch you are operating. When you make a commit, the commit is applied to a specific branch on which you are operating.

Step 5: Integrate branches

There are two ways to integrate branches: **Merge** and **Rebase**.

Merge is used to join two or more development histories together. You can merge branches by running **git merge** in your command line. Rebase is used to reapply commits on top of another base branch. The command to implement rebase is **git rebase**.

Both merge and rebase operations can be done on the GitHub platform. On GitHub, rebase is one option of the merge action. The merge operation on the GitHub platform will be explained in the next chapter.

Step 6: Manage conflicts

If there are changes in the same line of code on different branches, the Git system cannot merge those branches automatically. This situation is called **conflict**. You need to resolve conflicts before merging the branches. You can manually fix the lines of code to resolve conflicts.

Step 7: Delete an unused branch

A merged branch is not automatically deleted unless you delete it. After several branching and merging operations, you may see many unused branches in your repository. To delete a branch, you can use the **git branch -d [branch name]** command.

In the following pages, you'll learn how to manage branches in more detail.

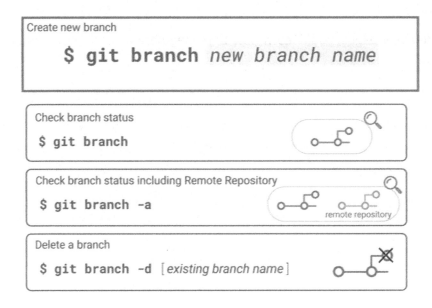

```
Create new branch
    $ git branch new branch name
```

```
Check branch status
$ git branch
```

```
Check branch status including Remote Repository
$ git branch -a
                                    remote repository
```

```
Delete a branch
$ git branch -d [existing branch name]
```

git branch is a multi-use command. We'll explain the three major use cases in this page.

The git branch command use cases

1. **Create a new branch**
2. **Check branch status**
3. **Delete an unused existing branch**

1. Create a new branch

Creating a new branch is the first action in the branch operation. When running **git branch [new branch name]**, a new branch is created from the original branch where you are located.

However, you are still on the original branch until you switch the current branch to the newly created branch by running the **git checkout** or **git switch** commands, which will be explained on the next pages.

Also, one important note here is that a new branch diverges from the latest commit (*HEAD*) of the parent branch. Unless you rebase it (to be explained later), the diverged point remains the same throughout the entire life cycle of the branch.

Example

If you want to create a new branch named *Branch_A*, run the command below.

```
git branch Branch_A
```

The image below illustrates an example of how *Branch_A* is created from the *master* branch.

```
$ git branch Branch_A
```
● Current branch

Create new branch

Branch_A

Master Branch

HEAD

Current branch is still under Master branch

2. Check branch status

When you simply run the **git branch** command without any additions, the command line returns the branch status. The branch status includes a list of branches and the information about which branch you are located in.

Example

In the following example, there are two branches: the *master* branch and *Branch_A*. The branch with " * " is the current branch, which is the *master* branch in this case.

Command Line - INPUT

```
git branch
```

Command Line - RESPONSE

```
  Branch_A
* master
```

The **git branch** command with the -a option returns the list of branches including branch information in the Remote Repository recorded in the Local Repository if the Local Repository is already linked with the Remote Repository.

Example

Command Line - INPUT

```
git branch -a
```

Command Line - RESPONSE

```
  Branch_A
* master
  remotes/origin/master
```

How to manage branches in the Remote Repository will be explained in the next chapter.

3. Delete unused branch

When you don't need a branch after merging it with another branch, you can delete the branch by running the **git branch -d [existing branch name]** command.

Example

Command Line - INPUT

```
git branch -d Branch_A
```

Command Line - RESPONSE

```
Deleted branch Branch_A (was 86c37e9).
```

If the branch you are trying to delete has not been merged with any other branches, the command line gives you an error.

Command Line - RESPONSE

```
error: The branch 'Branch_A' is not fully merged.
If you are sure you want to delete it, run 'git branch -D Branch_A'.
```

If you really want to delete the branch (for example, when you mistakenly made a new branch), you can use the **-D** option. **git branch -D [existing branch name]** allows you to delete a branch regardless of its merge history.

Example

Command Line - INPUT

```
git branch -D Branch_A
```

Command Line - RESPONSE

```
Deleted branch Branch_A (was b43edc9).
```

4. Rename branch

There are other usages of the **git branch** command. For example, if you want to change a branch name, you can use the **-m** option. Switch to the branch you want to rename. Then, run the **git branch -m [new branch name]** command.

Example

To change the *Branch_A*'s branch name to *Branch_B*, run the command below on *Branch_A*.

Command Line - INPUT

```
git branch -m Branch_B
```

Unless there is an error, the command line won't give you a response. To check if the branch name is successfully changed, run the **git branch** command.

Example

Command Line - INPUT

```
git branch
```

Command Line - RESPONSE

```
* Branch_B
  master
```

Switch Current Branch (1) – Git Checkout

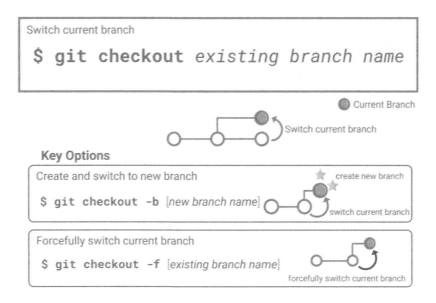

Switch current branch

```
$ git checkout existing branch name
```

◉ Current Branch

Switch current branch

Key Options

Create and switch to new branch

★ create new branch

```
$ git checkout -b [new branch name]
```

switch current branch

Forcefully switch current branch

```
$ git checkout -f [existing branch name]
```

forcefully switch current branch

The **git checkout** command is used for switching your current branch to a selected branch. You also create a new branch with the **-b** option and immediately switch to the new branch. When you switch your current branch with changes in *INDEX* and/ or the *Working Tree*, you need to carefully manage the operation as the changes may cause a problem.

Switch the current branch

As explained on the previous page, the **git branch [new branch name]** creates a new branch but the current branch location stays the same. **git checkout** is used when you want to switch your branch to a selected branch.

Example

To switch to *Branch_A*, run the command below.

Command Line - INPUT

git checkout Branch_A

Command Line - RESPONSE

Switched to branch 'Branch_A'

The image below illustrates an example of how the command above works.

$ git checkout Branch_A

● Current branch

Switch to new branch

Branch_A

Master Branch

Create a new branch and switch to the new branch

When you use this command with the **-b** option, you can create a new branch and switch to the new branch at the same time.

Example

To create a new branch named *Branch_A* and switch to the new branch at the same time, run the command below.

Command Line - INPUT

```
git checkout -b Branch_A
```

Command Line - RESPONSE

```
Switched to a new branch 'Branch_A'
```

The image below illustrates an example of how the command above works.

```
$ git checkout -b Branch_A
```
● Current branch

Create new branch

Branch_A

Master Branch

Switch to the new branch

Checkout when you have changes in INDEX and/or the working tree

When you checkout to another branch, the Git system tries to carry the changes in the *Working Tree* and *INDEX* over to the destination branch. If the latest commit statuses of both branches are the same, you can carry over the *Working Tree* and *INDEX* (*Situation A*).

Situation A: The latest commits are the same

● Current branch

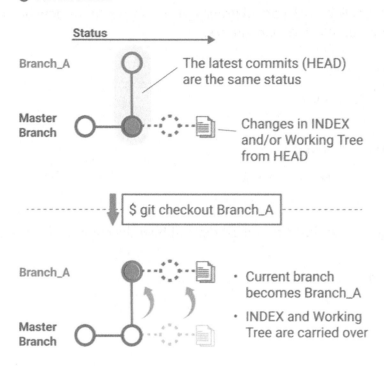

Status

Branch_A — The latest commits (HEAD) are the same status

Master Branch — Changes in INDEX and/or Working Tree from HEAD

$ git checkout Branch_A

Branch_A
• Current branch becomes Branch_A

Master Branch
• INDEX and Working Tree are carried over

However, if one of the branches has already evolved, you cannot switch to the destination branch (*Situation B*) ...

Situation B: The latest commits are different

● Current branch

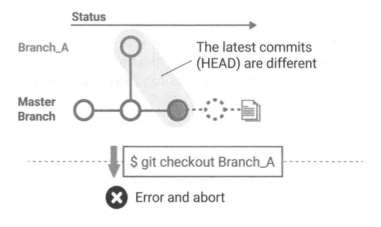

Status

Branch_A — The latest commits (HEAD) are different

Master Branch

$ git checkout Branch_A

❌ Error and abort

... and you'll see an error message like below.

> error: Your local changes to the following files would be overwritten by checkout:
>   git_practice.html
> Please commit your changes or stash them before you switch branches.
> Aborting

Solutions

There are some options to solve this issue.

Option 1. Commit all the changes and make the *INDEX, Working Tree*, and *HEAD* the same

Option 2. Stash the changes (refer to **Stash Changes - Git Stash**[4])

Option 3. Forcefully switch branches by running the **git checkout** command with the **-f** option

When you use the **-f** option, you need to be very careful as the *INDEX* and changes in the *Working Tree* are all cleared.

Practice

Developer A (Project Owner Role)

Objective:
Create, switch, and delete branches

1. Setup a practice project directory and file for this chapter

Directory and file structure

For this practice, we'll use the following directory and file. The directory and file will be used throughout the practices in this chapter except the last topic.

- Practice project directory: *git_branch_practice*
- *Practice file:* git_branch_practice.html

The screenshot below is the <u>target directory structure</u> example based on Mac OS.

---

4 https://d-libro.com/topic/stash-changes-git-stash

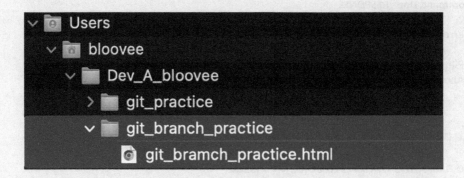

Create the practice project directory and file

Open the project's main directory (e.g., *Dev_A_bloovee*) with VS Code. You can use drag & drop to open the directory.

After opening the project's main directory with VS Code, open a new terminal in the VS Code window. The main project directory is already set as the current working directory in the command line.

You can also use the command line to move the current directory to the main project directory.

Command Line - INPUT

```
cd ~/Dev_A_bloovee
```

Once the current working directory is properly set, run the command below to create the directory and file.

```
mkdir git_branch_practice
cd git_branch_practice
touch git_branch_practice.html
```

Edit the practice HTML file

Open the *git_branch_practice.html* file with a text editor and make the following edits.

git_branch_practice.html (master)

```
<!doctype html>
<html lang="en">
<body>
<!-- Master Branch-->
<h1>M1</h1>
<!-- /Master Branch-->

<!-- Branch A-->
N/A
<!-- /Branch A-->

<!-- Branch B-->
N/A
<!-- /Branch B-->
</body>
```

For easier understanding, we'll add text for each branch in different lines of code dedicated to each branch. <!-- --> is used for making comments for html files. In the above case, we created three writing areas for each branch: *master*, *Branch_A*, and *Branch_B*. At this stage, only the *master* branch exists. For the *master* branch section, write "*M1*" under <h1> tag that will be the same as the commit message which we will create later on.

Create a Local Repository and make the first commit

After saving the file, commit the file with "*M1*" as a commit message. Run the following command to execute.

As we haven't initiated Git in the new project directory, run the **git init** command first. Add the files under the project directory to *INDEX* (in this case, only one file) and commit them. To check the commit status, run the **git log** command.

```
git init
git add .
git commit -m "M1"
git log --oneline
```

You can see that a new commit *"M1"* is created. (On Windows, you may not see the hint messages.)

Command Line - RESPONSE

```
hint: Using 'master' as the name for the initial branch. This default branch name
:
hint: git branch -m <name>
Initialized empty Git repository in
/Users/bloovee/Dev_A_bloovee/git_branch_practice/.git/
[master (root-commit) 8bf5c03] M1
1 file changed, 15 insertions(+)
create mode 100644 git_branch_practice.html
8bf5c03 (HEAD -> master) M1
```

Note: This approach is only for practice purposes. In actual projects, you need to use a concise description of the key changes in the code (e.g., *"fixed landing page UI"*, *"integrated APIs"*, etc.).

2. Create a new branch

Create *Branch_A* by running the **git branch Branch_A** command followed by the **git branch** to check the branch status.

Command Line - INPUT

```
git branch Branch_A
git branch
```

You can see that a new branch *Branch_A* has been created already, however, the current branch is still the *master* branch (the branch with asterisk " * " is the current branch):

Command Line - RESPONSE

```
  Branch_A
* master
```

3. Switch to the new branch

To make a new edit on the new branch, switch the current branch to *Branch_A* by running the **git checkout** command (you can also use the **git switch** command). Also, run the **git branch** command to confirm that the current branch has been switched to *Branch_A*.

Command Line - INPUT

```
git checkout Branch_A
git branch
```

You can see that the current branch has been switched to *Branch_A*:

Command Line - RESPONSE

```
Switched to branch 'Branch_A'
* Branch_A
  master
```

4. Edit and commit on the new branch (Branch_A)

To make another version of the project file, edit the *git_branch_practice.html* file. At this time, change only the *Branch_A* section of the file. Change *N/A* to *A1*, which will be the same as the first commit message on this branch.

git_branch_practice.html (Branch_A)

```
<!-- Branch A-->
<h1>A1</h1>
<!-- /Branch A-->
```

After saving the file, commit the file and check the log.

Command Line - INPUT

```
git commit -am "A1"
git log --oneline
```

You can see that a new commit has been created on *Branch_A*.

```
[Branch_A de11d0c] A1
 1 file changed, 1 insertion(+), 1 deletion(-)
de11d0c (HEAD -> Branch_A) A1
8bf5c03 (master) M1
```

5. Create a new branch and switch to the new branch with a shortcut

Go back to the *master* branch first to create another new branch from the *master* branch. To create *Branch_B* and switch to the branch using only one command, run **git checkout -b Branch_B** (or run **git switch -c Branch_B**). And check the branch status.

Command Line - INPUT

```
git checkout master
git checkout -b Branch_B
git branch
```

You can see that *Branch_B* has been created and it became the current branch.

Command Line - RESPONSE

```
Switched to branch 'master'
Switched to a new branch 'Branch_B'
  Branch_A
* Branch_B
  master
```

6. Edit and commit on the new branch (Branch_B)

To make another version of the project file, edit the *git_branch_practice.html* file again. This time, change only the *Branch_B* section of the file. Change *N/A* to *B1*, which will be the same as the first commit message on this branch.

git_branch_practice.html (Branch_B)

```
<!-- Branch B-->
<h1>B1</h1>
<!-- /Branch B-->
```

After saving the file, commit the file with a message of *"B1"* and check the log.

```
git commit -am "B1"
git log --oneline
```

You can see that a new commit was created on *Branch_B*. Although we have made a commit on *Branch_A*, we cannot see it in this log. This is because *Branch_B* diverged from the *master* branch (not from *Branch_A*).

Command Line - RESPONSE

```
[Branch_B 5536835] B1
 1 file changed, 1 insertion(+), 1 deletion(-)
5536835 (HEAD -> Branch_B) B1
8bf5c03 (master) M1
```

7. Forcefully switch to another branch

In the latest situation, you can switch to another branch as all changes are already committed (the *Working Tree* and *INDEX* are the same as *HEAD*). To create a situation where you cannot switch to another branch like in the case explained on the previous page, edit the practice file again and <u>save it</u> like shown below.

git_branch_practice.html (Branch_B)

```
<!-- Branch B-->
<h1>B1</h1>
<h1>B2</h1>
<!-- /Branch B-->
```

At this stage, the above edit is only reflected in the *Working Tree* and is not committed. Try to switch to *Branch_A* with the following command.

Command Line - INPUT

```
git checkout Branch_A
```

In this case, you'll see an error message like the one below.

Command Line - RESPONSE

```
error: Your local changes to the following files would be overwritten by checkout:
    git_branch_practice.html
Please commit your changes or stash them before you switch branches.
Aborting
```

Now try to switch to *Branch_A* with the "**-f**" option and check the branch status.

```
git checkout -f Branch_A
git branch
```

This time, you successfully switched to *Branch_A*, however, the changes done in the *Working Tree* are cleared by this command. You can check the status in your file.

```
Switched to branch 'Branch_A'
* Branch_A
  Branch_B
  master
```

The Branch B section is back to its original status.

git_branch_practice.html (Branch_A)

```
<!-- Branch B-->
N/A
<!-- /Branch B-->
```

8. Delete a branch

Lastly, delete *Branch_B*. As the branch has not been merged yet, so the "**-d**" option won't work. Use the "**-D**" option instead. Run the following commands and check the branch status.

```
git branch -D Branch_B
git branch
```

You can see that *Branch_B* has already been erased.

```
Deleted branch Branch_B (was 5536835).
* Branch_A
  master
```

For the next practice, let's also delete *Branch_A* by running the following commands.

Command Line - INPUT

```
git checkout master
git branch -D Branch_A
git branch
```

You can see that only the *master* branch exists.

Command Line - RESPONSE

```
Switched to branch 'master'
Deleted branch Branch_A (was de11d0c).
* master
```

Switch Current Branch (2) – Git Switch

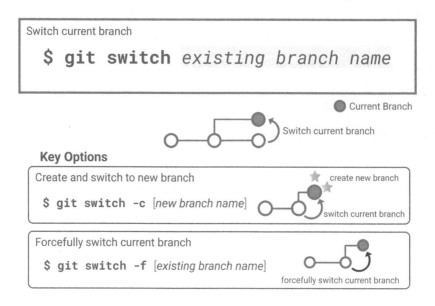

git switch is a newly introduced command as a substitute for the git checkout command. git switch returns the same result as git checkout.

Comparison between git checkout and git switch

These two commands are almost the same except for some option differences. For example, the -b option for git checkout is the -c option for git switch. Below are the key commands in comparison with the git checkout command.

Switch the current branch

- git switch [existing branch name]
- git checkout [existing branch name]

Create a new branch and switch to the new branch

- git switch -c [new branch name]
- git checkout -b [new branch name]

Forcefully switch to another branch

- **git switch -f [existing branch name]**
- **git checkout -f [existing branch name]**

Merge Branches – Git Merge

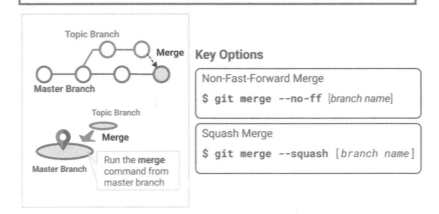

```
$ git merge target branch name
```

Key Options

Non-Fast-Forward Merge
```
$ git merge --no-ff [branch name]
```

Squash Merge
```
$ git merge --squash [branch name]
```

git merge is the command used when you want to merge branches. The merge operation can be done through the Remote Repository on the GitHub platform; it will be explained further in the next chapter.

When you run the **git merge** command, you need to run the command from the branch you want to continue to work on and specify a target branch name that you want to merge with the current branch.

There are four main cases for merge actions depending on the status of branches and command options.

1. **Fast-Forward Merge**
2. **Non-Fast-Forward Merge**
3. **Non-Fast Forward Merge with the "--no-ff" option**
4. **Squash Merge**

1. Fast-Forward Merge

When you are merging a child branch that is ahead of the parent branch (no changes were made to the parent branch after the point when you created the child branch), the **git merge** command simply brings changes made in the child branch into the parent branch without creating a new commit. In this case, the status of the branches will shift to the one shown in the following illustration.

This command moves the *HEAD* of the *master* branch forward to the point of the *HEAD* of *Branch_A*. The merge command doesn't impact *Branch_A*. The *master* branch simply becomes the same as the status of *Branch_A*.

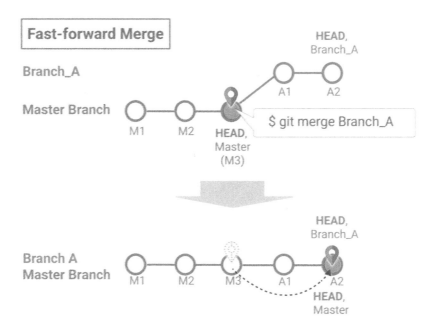

Key Points of Fast-Forward Merge

- **No new commit is created**
- **HEAD of the master branch moves forward to HEAD of Branch_A**
- **Branch_A still remains the same** (it is not deleted by the merge command)
- **The master branch and Branch_A reach the same status**

2. Non-Fast-Forward Merge

When the parent branch (e.g., *master* branch) is already ahead of the diverged point of the child branch, the merge action becomes a **non-fast-forward** merge. In this case, the merge action is recorded as a new commit. When you run the **git merge** command, a text editor is launched to add a commit message. A short description is already written in the text editor. You can change the message or just save it. When you close the editor, the merge action is completed. The following illustration describes the before and after of the **non-fast forward** merge.

In this case, the *HEAD* of the *master branch* moves forward integrating all commit histories under *Branch_A*.

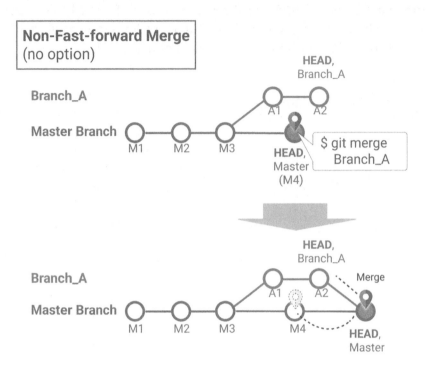

Key Points of Non-Fast Forward Merge

- **A new commit is created**
- **HEAD of the master branch moves forward while integrating the changes made in Branch_A**
- **Branch_A's commit histories are also recorded under the master branch**
- **Branch_A still remains the same** (it is not deleted by the merge command)

3. Non-Fast Forward Merge with the "--no-ff" option

Even when the status of branches is the same as the fast-forward case, you may want to create a new commit. If that is the case, you can use the **--no-ff** option. The command enforces the creation of the commit shown in the illustration below. The merge result becomes almost the same as the previous case; the only difference is that the previous case has commit *M4* before the *HEAD* on the master branch.

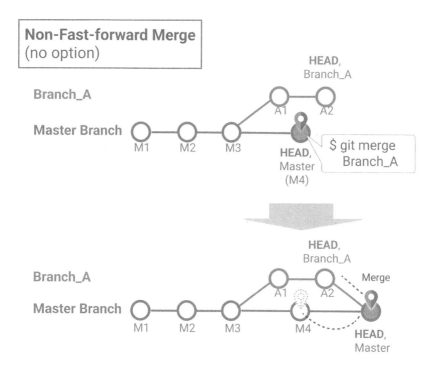

4. Squash Merge

Squash is another approach when you merge branches. This approach is useful when you don't want to keep every single detail of change histories in the *master* branch.

When you run the **git merge** command with the **--squash** option, all the changes made in the target branch are reflected in the destination branch. However, the command doesn't create a new commit. The changes are only reflected in the *Working Tree* and *INDEX* (see the illustration below).

When you want to proceed with the change, you need to make a new commit by running the **git commit** command. This command records only one new commit under the master branch. All commits under *Branch_A* are combined (**squashed**) in the new commit.

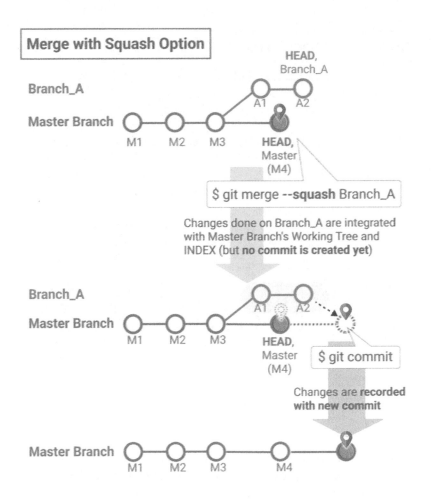

Merge with Squash Option

Branch_A

Master Branch
M1 M2 M3

HEAD, Branch_A
A1 A2

HEAD, Master (M4)

$ git merge --squash Branch_A

Changes done on Branch_A are integrated with Master Branch's Working Tree and INDEX (but **no commit is created yet**)

Branch_A

Master Branch
M1 M2 M3
A1 A2

HEAD, Master (M4)

$ git commit

Changes are **recorded with new commit**

Master Branch
M1 M2 M3 M4

Key Points of Squash Merge

- **No new commit is created by the git merge command**
- **The status of *Branch_A*** (the changes made after the divergence point from the master branch: commit *A1* and *A2*) **is integrated into the *Working Tree and INDEX* of the *master* branch**
- **You need to create a new commit to record the merge operation**
- ***Branch_A's* commit histories are not recorded under the master branch** (All commits under *Branch_A* are combined (**squashed**) in the new commit)
- ***Branch_A* still remains the same** (it is not deleted by the merge command)

Fast-Forward Merge

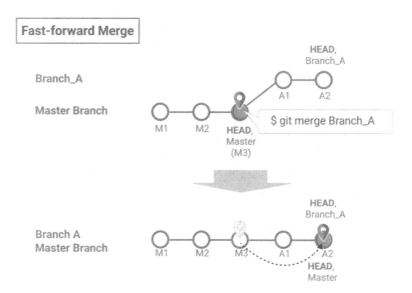

As explained, when you are merging a child branch that is simply ahead of the parent branch (no changes were made to the parent branch after the point when you created the child branch), the **git merge** command simply brings changes made in the child branch into the parent branch without creating a new commit. This merging approach is called **fast-forward merge**.

In the fast-forward merge, the status of the branches will shift to the one shown in the main figure. This command moves the *HEAD* of the *master* branch forward to the point of the *HEAD* of *Branch_A*. The merge command doesn't impact *Branch_A*. Simply, the *master* branch becomes the same as the status of *Branch_A*.

We'll explain the fast-forward merge in more detail with command line examples below.

Command Line Example

The command line image below is a demonstration of the commit and merge actions, which are the same as the upper illustration in the main figure. *M1*, *M2*, *M3*, *A1*, and *A2* are the commit messages that were already made before. We'll explain the commands and responses in the command line in four steps.

```
$ git log --oneline
a4c4eb0 (HEAD -> Branch_A) A2
62dda63 A1
e12beda (master) M3
f5ff7aa M2
8bf5c03 M1
```
①

```
$ git checkout master
Switched to branch 'master'

$ git merge Branch_A
Updating e12beda..a4c4eb0
Fast-forward
 git_branch_practice.html | 3 ++-
 1 file changed, 2 insertions(+), 1 deletion(-)
```
②

```
$ git log --oneline --graph
*a4c4eb0 (HEAD -> master, Branch_A) A2
*62dda63 A1
*e12beda M3
*f5ff7aa M2
*8bf5c03 M1
```
③

```
$ git checkout Branch_A
Switched to branch 'Branch_A'

$ git log --oneline
*a4c4eb0 (HEAD -> Branch_A, master) A2
*62dda63 A1
*e12beda M3
*f5ff7aa M2
*8bf5c03 M1
```
④

1. Confirm the original commit history status by running the **git log** command on *Branch_A*. You can see that the commit histories and branch statuses are the same as the ones illustrated in the main figure.

2. Switch to the *master* branch and run the **git merge Branch_A** command. You can see that this merge is **Fast-forward**.

3. Confirm how the commit history looks on the *master* branch by running the **git log** command. You can see that the *HEAD* of the *master* branch has moved forward to the same position as the *HEAD* of *Branch_A*.

4. To confirm the status of *Branch_A*, switch to *Branch_A* and run the **git log** command. You can see the same result as the one in the *master* branch. This means that *Branch_A* and the *master* branch are in the same status now.

For a better understanding, please go through the following practice section.

Practice

Developer A (Project Owner Role)

Objective:
Check how the Fast-Forward merge works

1. Prepare a practice file

In this practice, we'll modify the file and make some commits *M1*, *M2*, *M3*, *A1*, and *A2*. In the previous practice, we have already created the *git_branch_practice.html* file under the *git_branch_practice* directory. As we already deleted *Branch_A* and *Branch_B*, you have only the *master* branch now. The code on the *master* branch is like the one below.

git_branch_practice.html (master)

```
<!doctype html>
<html lang="en">
<body>
<!-- Master Branch-->
<h1>M1</h1>
<!-- /Master Branch-->

<!-- Branch_A-->
N/A
<!-- /Branch_A-->

<!-- Branch_B-->
N/A
<!-- /Branch_B-->
</body>
```

Make new commits on the master branch

To align with the upper illustration in the main figure, let's make commits *M2* and *M3* first.

Add *M2* under the html file and save it. Then, make a commit with "*M2*" as a commit message.

git_branch_practice.html (master)

```
<!-- Master Branch-->
<h1>M1</h1>
<h1>M2</h1>
<!-- /Master Branch-->
```

Command Line - INPUT

```
git commit -am "M2"
```

Command Line - RESPONSE

```
[master f5ff7aa] M2
 1 file changed, 1 insertion(+)
```

Repeat the same actions for commit *M3*.

git_branch_practice.html (master)

```
<!-- Master Branch-->
<h1>M1</h1>
<h1>M2</h1>
<h1>M3</h1>
<!-- /Master Branch-->
```

Command Line - INPUT

```
git commit -am "M3"
```

Command Line - RESPONSE

```
[master e12beda] M3
 1 file changed, 1 insertion(+)
```

Create a Branch_A and make new commits

Next, create *Branch_A* and checkout to this branch.

Command Line - INPUT

```
git checkout -b Branch_A
```

Command Line - RESPONSE

```
Switched to a new branch 'Branch_A'
```

To make commit *A1*, edit the file and save it first.

git_branch_practice.html (Branch_A)

```
<!-- Branch A-->
<h1>A1</h1>
<!-- /Branch A-->
```

Make commit *A1*.

Command Line - INPUT

```
git commit -am "A1"
```

Command Line - RESPONSE

```
[Branch_A 62dda63] A1
 1 file changed, 1 insertion(+), 1 deletion(-)
```

Repeat the same actions for commit *A2*.

git_branch_practice.html (Branch_A)

```
<!-- Branch A-->
<h1>A1</h1>
<h1>A2</h1>
<!-- /Branch A-->
```

Command Line - INPUT

```
git commit -am "A2"
```

Command Line - RESPONSE

```
[Branch_A a4c4eb0] A2
 1 file changed, 1 insertion(+)
```

Run the **git log** command to see the commit history.

Command Line - INPUT

```
git log --oneline
```

You'll see the following status shown below. Commit hash is a unique number generated by the computer each time. You'll see different ones on your computer, however, the structure of commit histories and branch status will be the same.

Command Line - RESPONSE

```
a4c4eb0 (HEAD -> Branch_A) A2
62dda63 A1
e12beda (master) M3
f5ff7aa M2
8bf5c03 M1
```

2. Perform the merge commit

As you need to run the merge command from the *master* branch, first switch the current branch to the *master* branch. Then, run the merge command.

Command Line - INPUT

```
git checkout master
git merge Branch_A
```

The command line response shows that the **Fast-forward** merge is executed.

Command Line - RESPONSE

```
switched to branch 'master'
Updating e12beda..a4c4eb0
Fast-forward
git_branch_practice.html | 3 ++-
  1 file changed, 2 insertions(+), 1 deletion(-)
```

3. Check commit histories and branch status

Check the status on the *master* branch first.

Command Line - INPUT

```
git log --oneline
```

You can see that the *HEAD* of the *master* branch moved forward to the same position as the *HEAD* of *Branch_A*. Also, you can confirm that no new commit is created by this operation.

```
a4c4eb0 (HEAD -> master, Branch_A) A2
62dda63 A1
e12beda M3
f5ff7aa M2
8bf5c03 M1
```

Next, check the status on *Branch_A*.

```
git checkout Branch_A
git log --oneline
```

You can see exactly the same results as the ones on the *master* branch. This means that the *master* branch and *Branch_A* are in the same status now.

```
a4c4eb0 (HEAD -> Branch_A, master) A2
62dda63 A1
e12beda M3
f5ff7aa M2
8bf5c03 M1
```

Non-Fast-Forward Merge (No Option)

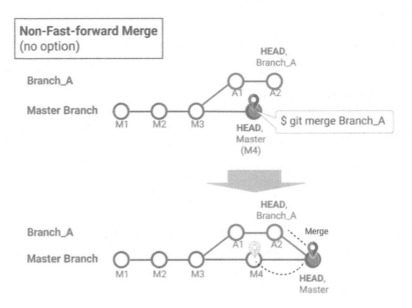

As explained, when the parent branch (e.g., *master* branch) is already ahead of the diverged point of the child branch, the merge action becomes a **non-fast-forward** merge. In this case, the merge action is recorded as a new commit.

The illustration in the main figure describes the before and after of the non-fast forward merge. In this case, the *HEAD* of the *master branch* moves forward integrating all commit histories under *Branch_A*.

We'll explain the non-fast-forward merge in more detail with command line examples below.

Command Line Example

The command line image below is a demonstration of the commit and merge actions, which are the same as the upper illustration in the main figure. *M1, M2, M3, A1,* and *A2* are the commit messages already made before this demonstration. We'll explain the commands and responses in the command line in three steps.

```
$ git log --oneline
b25d998 (HEAD -> master) M4
e12beda M3
f5ff7aa M2
8bf5c03 M1

$ git merge Branch_A
Auto-merging git_branch_practice.html
Merge made by the 'ort' strategy.
 git_branch_practice.html | 3 ++-
 1 file changed, 2 insertions(+), 1 deletion(-)

$ git log --oneline --graph
*   ececccc (HEAD -> master) Merge branch 'Branch_A'
|\
| * a4c4eb0 (Branch_A) A2
| * 62dda63 A1
* | b25d998 M4
|/
* e12beda M3
* f5ff7aa M2
* 8bf5c03 M1
```

1. Confirm the pre-merge commit history status by running the **git log** command on the *master* branch. You can see that the commit histories and branch statuses are the same as the ones illustrated in the main figure. (In this status, the merge operation done on the previous page has been reversed, and commit *M4* has already been added to demonstrate the non-fast-forward merge. Check the practice section below to see how to come to this status.)

2. Run the **git merge** command. When running the command, you'll see a temporary message on the command line saying "*hint: Waiting for your editor to close the file ...*" and a text editor is launched as shown in the image below. A commit message is already written there. If you want, you can modify the commit message. If you are fine with the message, save and close the file.

3. Check the branch status by running the **git log** command. You can see that the *HEAD* of the *master* branch is ahead of the *HEAD* of *Branch_A* as we created a new commit for the merge operation.

Example: commit message in a text editor

MERGE_MSG

Merge branch 'Branch_A'
Please enter a commit message to explain why this merge is necessary,
especially if it merges an updated upstream into a topic branch.
#
Lines starting with '#' will be ignored, and an empty message aborts
the commit.

251

(The Windows version of VS Code may not open the text editor. It may automatically create and save the commit message.)

For a better understanding, please go through the following practice section.

Practice

Developer A (Project Owner Role)

Objective:
Check how the Non-Fast-Forward merge (no option) works

1. Prepare a practice file

In the practice on the previous page, we already made commits *M1*, *M2*, and *M3* on the *master* branch and *A1* and *A2* on *Branch_A*. Also, *Branch_A* was merged into the *master* branch. For this practice purpose, we need to reverse the commit history before *Branch_A* was merged.

To reverse the *HEAD* of the *master* branch to commit *M3*, reset the merge operation by running the **git reset --hard** command on the *master* branch. Use the **commit hash** of commit *M3* which is generated on your computer. Also, make sure to use the **--hard** option. If you don't use the option, the statuses of the *Working Tree*, *INDEX*, and *HEAD* will be mixed.

Command Line - INPUT

```
git checkout master
git reset --hard e12beda
git log --oneline
```

You'll see that the *HEAD* of the *master* branch is back to Commit *M3*.

Command Line - RESPONSE

```
Switched to branch 'master'
HEAD is now at 3ad2537 M3
e12beda (HEAD -> master) M3
f5ff7aa M2
8bf5c03 M1
```

Next, create commit *M4* to align with the upper illustration on the main figure. Edit the html file (add "*<h1>M4</h1>*") and run the **git commit** command. To check the latest status, run the **git log** command again.

git_branch_practice.html (master)

```
<!-- Master Branch-->
<h1>M1</h1>
<h1>M2</h1>
<h1>M3</h1>
<h1>M4</h1>
<!-- /Master Branch-->
```

Command Line - INPUT

```
git commit -am "M4"
git log --oneline
```

Finally, you'll see the following status, which is aligned with the upper illustration on the main figure for the *master* branch.

Command Line - RESPONSE

```
b25d998 (HEAD -> master) M4
e12beda M3
f5ff7aa M2
8bf5c03 M1
```

As we haven't touched *Branch_A*, its status remains the same.

2. Perform the merge commit

Now you are ready to execute the merge command. As you are already on the *master* branch, run the following command.

Command Line - INPUT

```
git merge Branch_A
```

In the Non-Fast-forward case, the command line goes into the interactive mode while a text editor is launched. A text editor is used to write a commit message. A simple message is already written. Unless you want to add another message, you can close the text editor as it is.

Command Line - INTERACTIVE

Auto-merging git_branch_practice.html
hint: Waiting for your editor to close the file...

MERGE_MSG

Merge branch 'Branch_A'
Please enter a commit message to explain why this merge is necessary,
especially if it merges an updated upstream into a topic branch.
#
Lines starting with '#' will be ignored, and an empty message aborts
the commit.

Once you close the editor, the merge command is completed as shown below.

Command Line - RESPONSE

Merge made by the 'ort' strategy.
 git_branch_practice.html | 3 ++-
 1 file changed, 2 insertions(+), 1 deletion(-)

3. Check commit histories and branch status

Check the status of the *master* branch first. Add the "**--graph**" option this time as the branch status is slightly more complicated than the one in the previous example.

Command Line - INPUT

git log --oneline --graph

You can see that the *HEAD* of the *master* branch is ahead of the *HEAD* of *Branch_A*. Also, you can confirm that a new commit is created by this operation.

```
*   ececccc (HEAD -> master) Merge branch 'Branch_A'
|\
| * a4c4eb0 (Branch_A) A2
| * 62dda63 A1
* | b25d998 M4
|/
* e12beda M3
* f5ff7aa M2
* 8bf5c03 M1
```

Next, check the status of *Branch_A*.

Command Line - INPUT

```
git checkout Branch_A
git log --oneline
```

You can see that nothing has changed for *Branch_A*

Command Line - RESPONSE

```
a4c4eb0 (HEAD -> Branch_A) A2
62dda63 A1
e12beda M3
f5ff7aa M2
8bf5c03 M1
```

Non-Fast-Forward Merge (--no-ff Option)

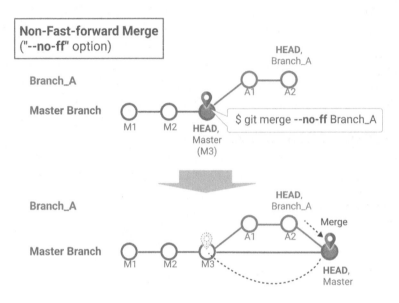

Even when the status of branches is the same as the fast-forward case, you may want to create a new commit. If that is the case, you can use the **--no-ff** option.

The command enforces the creation of the commit shown in the main figure. The merge result becomes almost the same as the case on the previous page; the only difference is that the previous case has commit *M4* before the *HEAD* on the master branch.

We'll explain how the non-fast-forward merge with the **--no-ff** option works in more detail with command line examples below.

Command Line Example

The command line image below is a demonstration of the commit and merge actions, which are the same as the upper illustration in the main figure. *M1*, *M2*, *M3*, *A1*, and *A2* are the commit messages which were already made before. We'll explain the commands and responses in the command line in three steps.

```
$ git log --oneline
e12beda (HEAD -> master) M3
f5ff7aa M2
8bf5c03 M1

$ git merge --no-ff Branch_A
Merge made by the 'ort' strategy.
 git_branch_practice.html | 3 ++-
 1 file changed, 2 insertions(+), 1 deletion(-)

$ git log --oneline --graph
*   73c7957 (HEAD -> master) Merge branch 'Branch_A'
|\
| * a4c4eb0 (Branch_A) A2
| * 62dda63 A1
|/
* e12beda M3
* f5ff7aa M2
* 8bf5c03 M1
```

1. Confirm the pre-merge commit history status by running the **git log** command on the *master* branch. You can see that the commit histories and branch statuses are the same as the ones illustrated in the main figure. (In this status, commit *M4* has already been erased from the last status on the previous page to demonstrate the non-fast-forward merge with the **--no-ff** option. Check the practice section below to see how to come to this status.)

2. Run the **git merge** command with the **--no-ff** option. When running the command, you'll see a temporary message on the command line saying "*hint: Waiting for your editor to close the file …*" and a text editor is launched as shown in the image below. A commit message is already written there. If you want, you can modify the commit message. If you are fine with the message, save and close the file.

3. Check the branch status by running the **git log** command. You can see that the *HEAD* of *master* is ahead of *HEAD* of *Branch_A* as we created a new commit for the merge operation.

Example: commit message in a text editor

MERGE_MSG

Merge branch 'Branch_A'
Please enter a commit message to explain why this merge is necessary,
especially if it merges an updated upstream into a topic branch.
#
Lines starting with '#' will be ignored, and an empty message aborts
the commit.

(The Windows version of VS Code may not open the text editor. It may automatically create and save the commit message.)

For a better understanding, please go through the following practice section.

Practice

Developer A (Project Owner Role)

Objective:
Check how the Non-Fast-Forward merge with the --no-ff option works

1. Prepare a practice file

In the practice on the previous page, we created commit *M4* on the *master* branch and merged *Branch_A* with the *master* branch. For this practice purpose, we need to reverse the commit history before *Branch_A* is merged.

To reverse the *HEAD* of the *master* branch to commit *M3*, reset the merge operation by running the **git reset --hard** command on the *master* branch. Use the **commit hash** of commit *M3* which is generated on your computer. Also, make sure to use the **--hard** option. If you don't use the option, the statuses of the *Working Tree*, *INDEX*, and *HEAD* will be mixed.

Command Line - INPUT

```
git checkout master
git reset --hard e12beda
git log --oneline
```

You'll see that the *HEAD* of the *master* branch is back to Commit *M3*, which is aligned with the upper illustration on the main figure for the *master* branch.

Command Line - RESPONSE

```
e12beda (HEAD -> master) M3
f5ff7aa M2
8bf5c03 M1
```

2. Perform the merge commit

Now you are ready to execute the merge command. As you are already on the *master* branch, run the following command with the **--no-ff** option.

```
git merge --no-ff Branch_A
```

As shown on the previous page, the command line goes into interactive mode while a text editor is launched. The text editor is used to write a commit message. A simple message is already written. Unless you want to modify the message, you can close the text editor as it is.

```
Auto-merging git_branch_practice.html
hint: Waiting for your editor to close the file...
```

```
Merge branch 'Branch_A'
# Please enter a commit message to explain why this merge is necessary,
# especially if it merges an updated upstream into a topic branch.
#
# Lines starting with '#' will be ignored, and an empty message aborts
# the commit.
```

Once you close the editor, the merge command is completed like below.

```
Merge made by the 'ort' strategy.
git_branch_practice.html | 3 ++-
 1 file changed, 2 insertions(+), 1 deletion(-)
```

3. Check commit histories and branch status

Check the status of the *master* branch first. Add the "--graph" option this time as the branch status is slightly more complicated than the one in the previous example.

259

```
git log --oneline --graph
```

You can see that the *HEAD* of the *master* branch is ahead of the *HEAD* of *Branch_A*. Also, you can confirm that a new commit is created by this operation. The only difference from the previous case (the Fast-forward no-option case) is that there is no *M4* commit and commit hash for the last commit.

Command Line - RESPONSE

```
*   73c7957 (HEAD -> master) Merge branch 'Branch_A'
|\
| * a4c4eb0 (Branch_A) A2
| * 62dda63 A1
|/
* e12beda M3
* f5ff7aa M2
* 8bf5c03 M1
```

Next, check the status of *Branch_A*.

Command Line - INPUT

```
git checkout Branch_A
git log --oneline
```

You can see that nothing has changed for *Branch_A*

Command Line - RESPONSE

```
a4c4eb0 (HEAD -> Branch_A) A2
62dda63 A1
e12beda M3
f5ff7aa M2
8bf5c03 M1
```

Squash Merge

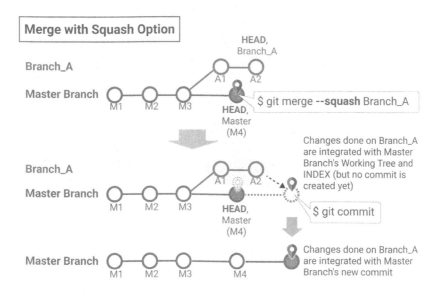

Squash merge is another approach when you merge branches. This approach is useful when you don't want to keep every single detail of change histories in the *master* branch.

When you run the **git merge** command with the **--squash** option, all the changes made in the target branch are reflected in the destination branch. However, the command doesn't create a new commit. The changes are only reflected in the *Working Tree* and *INDEX* (see the main figure).

When you want to proceed with the change, you need to make a new commit by running the **git commit** command. This command records only one new commit under the master branch. All commits under *Branch_A* are combined (**squashed**) in the new commit.

We'll explain squash merge with the **--squash** option in more detail with command line examples below.

Command Line Example

The command line image below is a demonstration of the commit and merge actions, which are the same as the upper illustration in the main figure. *M1, M2, M3, A1,* and *A2* are the commit messages that were already made before. We'll explain the commands and responses in the command line in six steps.

```
git log --oneline
b7b73d4 (HEAD -> master) M4
e12beda M3
f5ff7aa M2
8bf5c03 M1
```
①

```
$ git merge --squash Branch_A
Auto-merging git_branch_practice.html
Squash commit -- not updating HEAD
Automatic merge went well; stopped before committing
as requested
```
②

```
$ git status
On branch master
Changes to be committed:
  (use "git restore --staged <file>..." to unstage)
        modified:   git_branch_practice.html
```
③

```
$ git commit -am "Merge Branch_A (Squash)"
[master ef8b675] Merge Branch_A (Squash)
 1 file changed, 2 insertions(+), 1 deletion(-)
```
④

```
$ git log --oneline --graph
* 161bc6c (HEAD -> master) Merge Branch_A (Squash)
* b7b73d4 M4
* e12beda M3
* f5ff7aa M2
* 8bf5c03 M1
```
⑤

```
$ git checkout Branch_A
Switched to branch 'Branch_A'

$git log --oneline --graph
* a4c4eb0 (HEAD -> Branch_A) A2
* 62dda63 A1
* e12beda M3
* f5ff7aa M2
* 8bf5c03 M1
```
⑥

1. Confirm the pre-merge commit history status by running the **git log** command on the *master* branch. You can see that the commit histories and branch statuses are the same as the ones illustrated in the main figure. (In this status, the merge operation done on the previous page has been reversed, and commit *M4* has already been added to demonstrate the squash merge. Check the practice section below to see how to come to this status.)

2. Run the **git merge** command with the **--squash** option. When running the command with the option, no commit is created. The command reflects the changes made on *Branch_A* in the *Working Tree* and *INDEX*.

3. To confirm that the changes have not yet been committed on the *master* branch, run the **git status** command. You'll see a modified file under the *INDEX*. To understand what changes were made to the file, you can see an example in the image below (Working Tree File Status). You can see that the working file on the *master* branch has become an integrated version of the *master* branch (before squash) and *Branch_A*.

4. To make a record of the change, run the **git merge** command.

5. To check the latest branch status, run the **git log** command on the *master* branch. You can see that a new commit is created, however, there are no *A1* and *A2* in the commit history. This means that the squash option combined (squashed) all the changes made to the merging branch to simplify the line of commit history.

6. To check the latest status of *Branch_A*, switch to *Branch_A* and run the **git log** command. You can see that nothing has changed on *Branch_A*

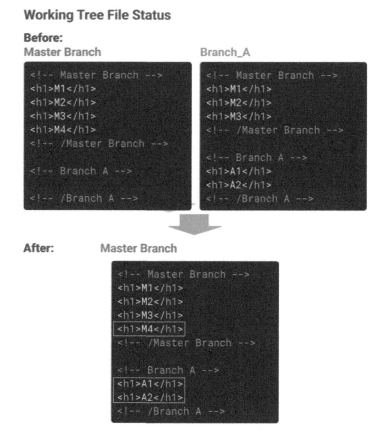

Working Tree File Status

Before:

Master Branch

```
<!-- Master Branch -->
<h1>M1</h1>
<h1>M2</h1>
<h1>M3</h1>
<h1>M4</h1>
<!-- /Master Branch -->

<!-- Branch A -->

<!-- /Branch A -->
```

Branch_A

```
<!-- Master Branch -->
<h1>M1</h1>
<h1>M2</h1>
<h1>M3</h1>
<!-- /Master Branch -->

<!-- Branch A -->
<h1>A1</h1>
<h1>A2</h1>
<!-- /Branch A -->
```

After: Master Branch

```
<!-- Master Branch -->
<h1>M1</h1>
<h1>M2</h1>
<h1>M3</h1>
<h1>M4</h1>
<!-- /Master Branch -->

<!-- Branch A -->
<h1>A1</h1>
<h1>A2</h1>
<!-- /Branch A -->
```

For a better understanding, please go through the following practice section.

Practice

Objective:

Check how the squash merge works

1. Prepare a practice file

In the practice on the previous page, *Branch_A* was already merged into the *master* branch. For this practice purpose, we need to reverse the commit history before *Branch_A* is merged.

To reverse the *HEAD* of the *master* branch to commit *M3*, reset the merge operation by running the **git reset --hard** command on the *master* branch. Use the **commit hash** of commit *M3* which is generated on your computer. Also, make sure to use the **--hard** option. If you don't use the option, the statuses of the *Working Tree*, *INDEX*, and *HEAD* will be mixed.

Command Line - INPUT

```
git checkout master
git reset --hard e12beda
git log --oneline
```

You'll see that the *HEAD* of the *master* branch is back to Commit *M3*.

Command Line - RESPONSE

```
e12beda (HEAD -> master) M3
f5ff7aa M2
8bf5c03 M1
```

Next, create commit *M4* to match the upper illustration on the main figure. Edit the HTML file (add *<h1>M4</h1>* and run the **git commit** command. To check the latest status, run the **git log** command again.

git_branch_practice.html

```
<!-- Master Branch-->
<h1>M1</h1>
<h1>M2</h1>
<h1>M3</h1>
<h1>M4</h1>
<!-- /Master Branch-->
```

Command Line - INPUT

```
git commit -am "M4"
git log --oneline
```

Finally, you'll see the following *master* branch status, which matches the upper illustration on the main figure. As we haven't touched *Branch_A*, its status remains the same.

Command Line - RESPONSE

```
b7b73d4 (HEAD -> master) M4
e12beda M3
f5ff7aa M2
8bf5c03 M1
```

2. Perform squash merge

Now you are ready to execute the merge command. As you are already on the *master* branch, run the following command with the **--squash** option.

Command Line - INPUT

```
git merge --squash Branch_A
```

In this case, no commit is made as you can see the response in the command line like shown below.

Command Line - RESPONSE

```
Auto-merging git_branch_practice.html
Squash commit -- not updating HEAD
Automatic merge went well; stopped before committing as requested
```

Instead, changes made on *Branch_A* are reflected in the *Working Tree* of the *master* branch shown in the text editor below.

git_branch_practice.html

```
<!doctype html>
<html lang="en">
<body>
<!-- Master Branch-->
<h1>M1</h1>
<h1>M2</h1>
<h1>M3</h1>
<h1>M4</h1>
<!-- /Master Branch-->

<!-- Branch_A-->
<h1>A1</h1>
<h1>A2</h1>
<!-- /Branch_A-->

<!-- Branch_B-->
N/A
<!-- /Branch_B-->
</body>
```

The changes are also staged. To check the status, run the **git status** command.

Command Line - INPUT

```
git status
```

You can see that *git_branch_practice.html* was modified and staged (ready to commit).

Command Line - RESPONSE

```
On branch master
Changes to be committed:
    (use "git restore --staged <file>..." to unstage)
        modified:   git_branch_practice.html
```

2. Make a commit

As the **git merge --squash** command doesn't create a new commit in a normal setting, you need to run the **git commit** command to make a record like below.

```
git commit -am "Merge Branch_A (Squash)"
```

You can see that a new commit is created like shown below.

```
[master 161bc6c] Merge Branch_A (Squash)
 1 file changed, 2 insertions(+), 1 deletion(-)
```

3. Check commit histories and branch status

Check the status of the *master* branch first.

```
git log --oneline --graph
```

You can see that a new commit is created, however, there are no *A1* and *A2* in the commit history. This means that the squash option combined (squashed) all the changes made to the merging branch to simplify the line of commit history.

```
* 161bc6c (HEAD -> master) Merge Branch_A (Squash)
* b7b73d4 M4
* e12beda M3
* f5ff7aa M2
* 8bf5c03 M1
```

Next, check the status on *Branch_A*.

```
git checkout Branch_A
git log --oneline --graph
```

You can see that nothing has changed for *Branch_A*

Command Line - RESPONSE

* a4c4eb0 (HEAD -> Branch_A) A2
* 62dda63 A1
* e12beda M3
* f5ff7aa M2
* 8bf5c03 M1

Rebase Branch – Git Rebase

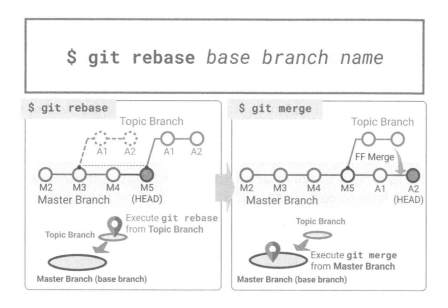

git rebase is the command used to reapply all the commits made on the topic branch on top of the *HEAD* of the **base branch** (the branch that the topic branch was separated from). This command is useful when you want to streamline commits made on multiple branches. The rebase operation can also be done through a Remote Repository on the GitHub platform. It is an option of the **merge** feature of GitHub.

In the command line, you need to run the command on the branch to be rebased (a divergent branch) and specify its base branch name as a command parameter.

```
git rebase [base branch name]
```

The rebase command changes the divergence point to the *HEAD* of the base branch. It doesn't impact the base branch itself. If you want to integrate the changes into the base branch (e.g., the *master* branch), you need to run the **git merge** command on the base branch side. The merge action will be the **Fast-Forward** merge as the divergent branch is already ahead of the *HEAD* of the base branch.

For a better understanding, please go through the following practice section.

Practice

Objective:
Learn how to rebase a branch

1. Prepare a practice file

In the practice on the previous page, we merged *Branch_A* with the *master* branch using the squash option. For this practice purpose, we need to reverse the commit history before *Branch_A* was merged.

To reverse the *HEAD* of the *master* branch to commit *M4*, reset the merge operation by running the **git reset --hard** command on the *master* branch. Use the **commit hash** of commit *M4* which is generated on your computer. Also, make sure to use the **--hard** option. If you don't use the option, the statuses of the *Working Tree*, *INDEX*, and *HEAD* will be mixed.

Command Line - INPUT

```
git checkout master
git reset --hard b7b73d4
git log --oneline
```

You'll see that the *HEAD* of the *master* branch is back to Commit *M4*.

Command Line - RESPONSE

```
b7b73d4 (HEAD -> master) M4
e12beda M3
f5ff7aa M2
8bf5c03 M1
```

Next, create commit *M5* to match the illustration on the left of the main figure. Edit the HTML file (add *<h1>M5</h1>* and run the **git commit** command. To check the latest status, run the **git log** command again.

270

git_branch_practice.html

```
<!-- Master Branch-->
<h1>M1</h1>
<h1>M2</h1>
<h1>M3</h1>
<h1>M4</h1>
<h1>M5</h1>
<!-- /Master Branch-->
```

Command Line - INPUT

```
git commit -am "M5"
git log --oneline
```

Finally, you'll see the following status, which matches the illustration on the left of the main figure for the *master* branch.

Command Line - RESPONSE

```
288068f (HEAD -> master) M5
b7b73d4 M4
e12beda M3
f5ff7aa M2
8bf5c03 M1
```

Check the status of *Branch_A*.

Command Line - INPUT

```
git checkout Branch_A
git log --oneline
```

As we haven't touched *Branch_A* in this practice yet, its status remains the same as the one in the previous practice. *Branch_A* has diverged at commit *M3* of the *master* branch, which is aligned with the original position of the Topic Branch on the illustration on the left of the main figure.

```
a4c4eb0 (HEAD -> Branch_A) A2
62dda63 A1
e12beda M3
f5ff7aa M2
8bf5c03 M1
```

2. Run the rebase command

Now you are ready to execute the rebase command. As you are already on *Branch_A*, run the following command.

Command Line - INPUT

```
git rebase master
```

You can see that *Branch_A* was successfully rebased.

Command Line - RESPONSE

```
Successfully rebased and updated refs/heads/Branch_A.
```

To check the latest status of *Branch_A*, run the **git log** command.

Command Line - INPUT

```
git log --oneline
```

Now you can see that *Branch_A* was rebased to the *HEAD* of the *master* branch (commit *M5*). In this operation, you can also confirm that the commit hashes for commits *A1* and *A2* are different from the original ones although the committed file versions remain the same.

```
479f994 (HEAD -> Branch_A) A2
6d96103 A1
288068f (master) M5
b7b73d4 M4
e12beda M3
f5ff7aa M2
8bf5c03 M1
```

3. Run the merge command

The rebase command changed the *Branch_A* status, however, the *master* branch stays the same; its *HEAD* is still at commit *M5*.

Command Line - INPUT

```
git checkout master
git log --oneline
```

Command Line - RESPONSE

```
288068f (HEAD -> master) M5
b7b73d4 M4
e12beda M3
f5ff7aa M2
8bf5c03 M1
```

If you want to integrate the change in *Branch_A* into the *master* branch, you need to run the merge command.

Command Line - INPUT

```
git merge Branch_A
```

In this case, the merge operation becomes Fast-forward as *Branch_A* was reattached to the *HEAD* of the master.

Command Line - RESPONSE

```
Updating 288068f..479f994
Fast-forward
 git_branch_practice.html | 3 ++-
 1 file changed, 2 insertions(+), 1 deletion(-)
```

To check the latest status of the *master* branch, run the **git log** command.

Command Line - INPUT

```
git log --oneline
```

Now you can see that the *HEAD* of the *master* branch moved forward to the same position as the *HEAD* of *Branch_A*; the statuses of the *master* branch and *Branch_A* became the same.

Command Line - RESPONSE

```
479f994 (HEAD -> master, Branch_A) A2
6d96103 A1
288068f M5
b7b73d4 M4
e12beda M3
f5ff7aa M2
8bf5c03 M1
```

Managing Conflict

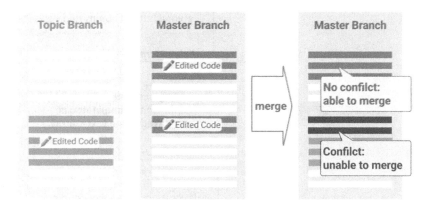

— Git gives us an alert when there is any conflict
— When a conflict happens, it needs to be resolved before merging branches

If you work with another developer on the same project and edit the same file on different branches simultaneously, both of you may change the same line in the same file. In this case, it is hard to judge which one becomes the master code. This situation is called **conflict**.

Another case of conflict is the case where one developer deletes a file while another developer continued working on the file.

If you try to merge the branches with a conflict, the Git system won't be able to complete the merge operation automatically. In that case, the Git system creates an alert identifying the location of the conflict through the registered text editor.

The flow chart below illustrates the typical workflow when you run the **git merge** command.

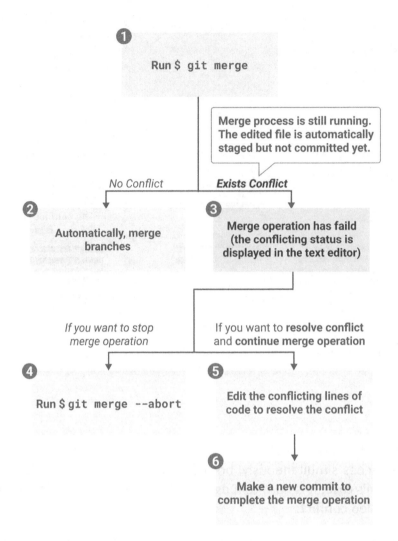

1. Run the **git merge** command to trigger the merge process.

2. When there is no conflict, the Git system automatically completes the merge process.

3. When there is a conflict, the Git system suspends the automatic merge process. At this point, the merge process is still running manually; the edited files are staged during this process so that the files are ready to be committed.

4. If you want to stop the merge operation, run the **git merge --abort** command. When you run the command, the merge operation is aborted and the status of working files and branches will be reverted to the status they had before running the **git merge** command

5. If you want to resolve the conflict and continue the merge operation, edit the conflicting lines of code to resolve the conflict.

Options to solve a conflict

To resolve the conflict, the Git system suggests four options through the registered text editor like shown in the image below. If you click one of the first three options, the changes are reflected in the text editor. If you click the last "Compare Changes" option, a read-mode text editor launches to show the comparison of the two branches.

1. **Accept Current Change** (Keep the changes on the branch where you are executing the merge command)

2. **Accept Incoming Change** (Keep the changes on the branch being merged)

3. **Accept Both** (Keep both changes)

4. **Compare Changes**

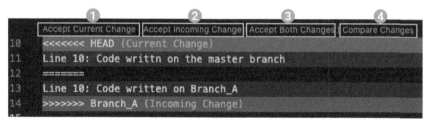

- Four options are listed in text editor
- You can click one of the options to execute

1. Accept Current Change
2. Accept Incoming Change
3. Accept Both Changes
4. Compare Changes

If none of the options **1** - **3** gives what you want, you can also edit the code further to customize the conflict resolution.

6. Once the conflict is resolved, you can run the **git commit** command to complete the merge operation

For a better understanding, please go through the following practice section.

Practice

Objective:
Solve a conflict

1. Prepare a practice file: create a conflict

At the end of the practice on the previous page, the *master* branch and *Branch_A* reached the same status. Check the latest status by running the **git log** command.

Command Line - INPUT

```
git log --oneline
```

You'll see that the *HEAD* of both the *master* branch and *Branch_A* is commit *A2*.

Command Line - RESPONSE

```
479f994 (HEAD -> master, Branch_A) A2
6d96103 A1
288068f M5
b7b73d4 M4
e12beda M3
f5ff7aa M2
8bf5c03 M1
```

To create a conflict, first, revert the *master* branch to commit *M5* by running the **git reset --hard** command. Use the commit hash of commit *M5* which is generated on your computer. Also, make sure to use the **--hard** option. If you don't use the option, the statuses of the *Working Tree*, Staging Area and *HEAD* will be mixed up.

Command Line - INPUT

```
git reset --hard 288068f
git log --oneline
```

You'll see that the *HEAD* of the *master* branch is back to Commit *M5*.

```
HEAD is now at 1923334 M5
288068f (HEAD -> master) M5
b7b73d4 M4
e12beda M3
f5ff7aa M2
8bf5c03 M1
```

Next, edit the file like below by adding *<h1>M6</h1>* after *<!-- Branch_A-->*, which is supposed to be the editing area for *Branch_A*. <u>After saving the file</u>, run the **git commit** command.

git_branch_practice.html

```
<!-- Branch_A-->
<h1>M6</h1>
<!-- /Branch_A-->
```

Command Line - INPUT

```
git commit -am "M6"
git log --oneline
```

You can see that the *HEAD* of the *master* branch is now at commit *M6*.

Command Line - RESPONSE

```
44614a9 (HEAD -> master) M6
288068f M5
b7b73d4 M4
e12beda M3
f5ff7aa M2
8bf5c03 M1
```

2. Run the merge command: confirm a conflict

Now you can run the merge command expecting there is a conflict.

```
git merge Branch_A
```

You'll see a message saying "Automatic merge failed" in the command line.

```
Auto-merging git_branch_practice.html
CONFLICT (content): Merge conflict in git_branch_practice.html
Automatic merge failed; fix conflicts and then commit the result.
```

Also, a text editor (VS Code) is opened when you encounter a conflict indicating the location of the conflict as shown below.

git_branch_practice.html

```
<!-- Branch_A-->
<<<<<<< HEAD (Current Change)
<h1>M6</h1>
=======
<h1>A1</h1>
<h1>A2</h1>
>>>>>>> Branch_A (Incoming Change)
<!-- /Branch_A-->
```

3. Resolve a conflict

VS Code editor shows some options to resolve the conflict. Also, the editor shows the **Resolve in Merge Editor** button at the bottom. You can select one of the options or press the button.

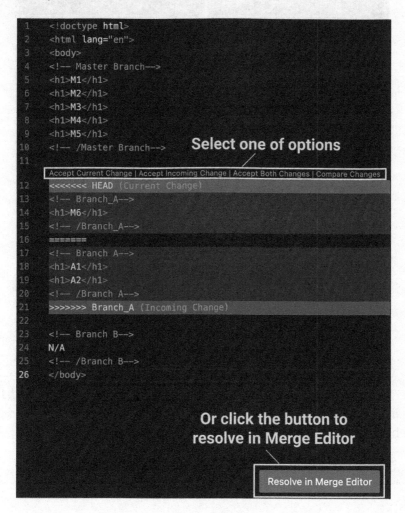

In this practice, we use the Merge Editor. When you press the **Resolve in Merge Editor** button, you'll see the comparison between the Incoming change and the Current change with the editing area at the bottom as shown below.

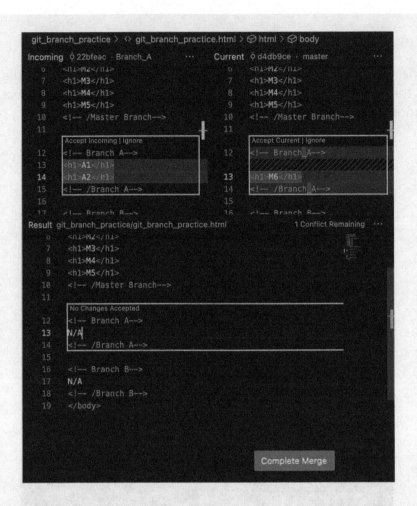

To solve the conflict, we'll move *<h1>M6</h1>* to after *<h1>M5</h1>* while keeping incoming change (edits on *Branch_A*). The edited code should look like the one below.

git_branch_practice.html

```html
<!-- Master Branch-->
<h1>M1</h1>
<h1>M2</h1>
<h1>M3</h1>
<h1>M4</h1>
<h1>M5</h1>
<h1>M6</h1>
<!-- /Master Branch-->

<!-- Branch_A-->
<h1>A1</h1>
<h1>A2</h1>
<!-- /Branch_A-->
```

Once the edit is done, press the **Complete Merge** button.

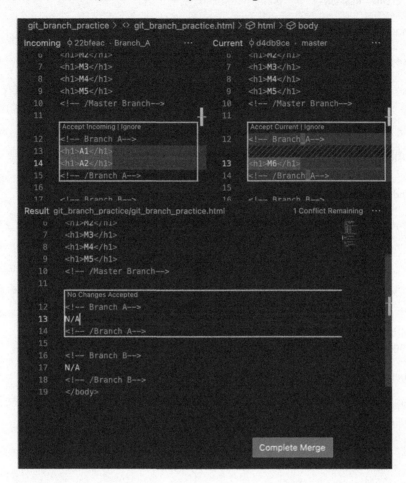

At this stage, the change is not reflected in any commit. To check the status, run the **git status** command.

Command Line - INPUT

```
git status
```

You can see that the merged code has not been committed yet.

To complete the merge operation, make a new commit.

Now you can see that *Branch_A* was successfully merged with the *master* branch.

The demo code is available in this repository (**Demo Code**[5]).

---

5 https://github.com/git-github-introduction/git_branch_practice

Stash Changes – Git Stash

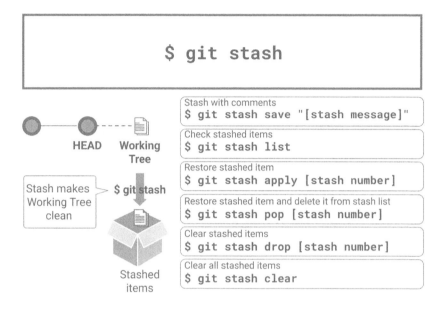

```
$ git stash
```

HEAD   Working
        Tree

Stash makes
Working Tree $ git stash
clean

Stashed
items

Stash with comments
```
$ git stash save "[stash message]"
```

Check stashed items
```
$ git stash list
```

Restore stashed item
```
$ git stash apply [stash number]
```

Restore stashed item and delete it from stash list
```
$ git stash pop [stash number]
```

Clear stashed items
```
$ git stash drop [stash number]
```

Clear all stashed items
```
$ git stash clear
```

git stash is used to separately manage work-in-progress (WIP) codes. When you want to switch the current branch in the middle of editing the *Working Tree* and *INDEX*, the edits can prevent you from switching the current branch (refer to the **git checkout** page). In that case, the **git stash** command is useful. The stashed lines of code are parked somewhere temporarily and make the *Working Tree* and *INDEX* clean (the *Working Tree* and *INDEX* statuses become the same as the *HEAD* status) so that you can switch branches.

Key Git Stash Commands

- **git stash**: stash the *Working Tree* and *INDEX*
- **git stash save "[stash message]"**: stash the *Working Tree* and *INDEX* with a stash message
- **git stash list**: list up stashed items
- **git stash apply [stash number]**: restore a stashed item
- **git stash pop [stash number]**: restore a stashed item and delete it from the stash list
- **git stash drop [stash number]**: delete a stashed item
- **git stash clear**: delete all the stashed items

For a better understanding, please go through the following practice section.

git_branch_stash_practice.html (master)

```html
<!doctype html>
<html lang="en">
<body>
<!-- Master Branch-->
<h1>M1</h1>
<!-- /Master Branch-->

<!-- Branch A-->
N/A
<!-- /Branch A-->

<!-- Branch B-->
N/A
<!-- /Branch B-->
</body>
```

<u>After saving the file</u>, commit the file with *"M1"* as a commit message. Run the following command to execute.

As we haven't initiated Git in the new project directory, run the **git init** command first.

Command Line - INPUT

```
git init
git add .
git commit -m "M1"
```

For Branch_A

Create and checkout to *Branch_A*.

Command Line - INPUT

```
git checkout -b Branch_A
```

Command Line - RESPONSE

```
Switched to new branch 'Branch_A'
```

To make another version of the project file, edit the HTML file.

git_branch_stash_practice.html (Branch_A)

```html
<!-- Branch A-->
<h1>A1</h1>
<!-- /Branch A-->
```

After saving the file, commit the file and check the log.

Command Line - INPUT

```
git commit -am "A1"
git log --oneline
```

You can see that a new commit has been created on *Branch_A*.

Command Line - RESPONSE

```
[Branch_A 466f3af] A1
  1 file changed, 1 insertion(+), 1 deletion(-)
466f3af (HEAD -> Branch_A) A1
9d2bd84 (master) M1
```

You can also clone this repository to create the above practice directory and file (**Demo Code**[6]).

---

6 https://github.com/git-github-introduction/git_branch_stash_practice

2. Make WIP code

To test the **git stash** command, edit the file on the *master* branch shown below and save the file, but do not commit it. Switch to the *master* branch.

```
git checkout master
```

Edit the file by adding *<h1>M2</h1>*.

git_branch_stash_practice.html (master)

```
<!-- Master Branch-->
<h1>M1</h1>
<h1>M2</h1>
<!-- /Master Branch-->

<!-- Branch_A-->
N/A
<!-- /Branch_A-->
```

At this stage, the *Working Tree* is already ahead of the *HEAD* (the latest commit) of the master branch. As explained, you cannot switch to *Branch_A*. You can confirm it by running the **git checkout** command.

Command Line - INPUT

```
git checkout Branch_A
```

You'll get an error message like the one below.

Command Line - RESPONSE

```
error: Your local changes to the following files would be overwritten by checkout:
    git_branch_stash_practice.html
Please commit your changes or stash them before you switch branches.
Aborting
```

The command line response suggests two options before you switch branches.

- **Commit the changes**
- **Stash the changes**

3. Run the stash command: $ git stash

First, test the **git stash** command.

Command Line - INPUT

```
git stash
```

You'll see the following message.

Command Line - RESPONSE

```
Saved working directory and index state WIP on master: 462ee77 M1
```

When you run the stash command, the editing file in the *Working Tree* is reverted to *HEAD* (the latest commit).

git_branch_stash_practice.html (master)

```
<!-- Master Branch-->
<h1>M1</h1>
<!-- /Master Branch-->
```

Now you can switch to *Branch_A* like shown below.

Command Line - INPUT

```
git checkout Branch_A
```

You'll see the following message.

Command Line - RESPONSE

```
Switched to branch 'Branch_A'
```

4. Check the stash status: $ git stash list

To check the list of stashed items, run the **git stash list** command.

```
git stash list
```

You can see that one item is stashed. **stash@{0}** is a stash number that is used when you restore the stashed item.

```
stash@{0}: WIP on master: 462ee77 M1
```

5. Restore a stashed item: $ git stash apply or $ git stash pop

To restore a stashed item, you have two options:

Option 1: $ git stash apply

The **git stash apply** command simply restores the stashed item.

Option 2: $ git stash pop

When you run the **git stash pop** command, it restores the stashed item and deletes the stashed item from the stashed list.

In this practice, we use the **git stash apply** command. You can run the command with or without a stash number. If you don't put in the stash number, the latest stash is restored. Before running the command, switch back to the master branch first to see the simplest case.

Note: You can restore the stashed items to other branches, however, this may create a conflict.)

```
git checkout master
git stash apply
```

You can see that the file status is back to the one before you run the stash command as shown below.

git_branch_stash_practice.html (master)

```
<!-- Master Branch-->
<h1>M1</h1>
<h1>M2</h1>
<!-- /Master Branch-->
```

On the command line, you can see a message like the one below. This is the same response you get when you run the **git status** command.

Command Line - RESPONSE

```
On branch master
Changes not staged for commit:
    (use "git add <file>..." to update what will be committed)
    (use "git restore <file>..." to discard changes in working directory)
        modified: git_branch_stash_practice.html

no changes added to commit (use "git add" and/or "git commit -a")
```

6. Delete a stashed item: $ git stash drop or $ git clear

When you don't need the stashed item anymore, you can delete it. To delete one stashed item, you can use **git stash drop [stash number]**. If you want to clear all the stashed items, you can use **git stash clear**. In this practice, we use **git stash drop**. If you don't specify a stash number, the command deletes the latest stash.

Command Line - INPUT

```
git stash drop
```

You'll see a message like below.

```
Dropped refs/stash@{0} (887b349943b8fddd3798cb7fb5e714bf4e1e1ebd))
```

7. Manage multiple stash items

When you create multiple stashed items, you may be confused about what each stash number means. To avoid confusion, you can add a simple stash message when you stash changes by running the **git stash save "[stash message]"** command.

Command Line - INPUT

```
git stash save "M2"
```

You'll see a message like below.

Command Line - RESPONSE

```
Saved working directory and index state On master: M2
```

As you stashed, the *Working Tree* is cleared as shown below.

git_branch_stash_practice.html (master)

```html
<!-- Master Branch-->
<h1>M1</h1>
<!-- /Master Branch-->
```

Create other stashed items

Edit the HTML file again by adding *<h1>M3</h1>* this time.

git_branch_stash_practice.html (master)

```html
<!-- Master Branch-->
<h1>M1</h1>
<h1>M3</h1>
<!-- /Master Branch-->
```

After saving the file, run the **git stash save** command with a stash message of *"M3"*.

Command Line - INPUT

git stash save "M3"

Repeat the same process for *M4* and *M5*. And check the stash list.

Command Line - INPUT

git stash list

You can see that the four stashed items are created as shown below.

Command Line - RESPONSE

stash@{0}: On master: M5
stash@{1}: On master: M4
stash@{2}: On master: M3
stash@{3}: On master: M2

The stash message is useful especially when you delete stashed items as stash numbers can change when you delete stashed items. Try the following commands to see the result.

Command Line - INPUT

git stash drop
git stash list

You can see that **stash@{0}** now refers to *M4* while it was previously referred to as *M5*.

Command Line - RESPONSE

Dropped refs/stash@{0} (4b5d38036ccdf8a0e0284255b5de9a53882e0d63)
stash@{0}: On master: M4
stash@{1}: On master: M3
stash@{2}: On master: M2

Chapter 6

Remote Collaboration

Remote Collaboration – Git & GitHub One of the key features of Git is that it allows collaboration with others. You can share your code through a remote repository with your team members and vice versa.

One of the key features of Git is that it allows collaboration with others. You can share your code through a Remote Repository with your team members and vice versa. This chapter will explain how to collaborate with others in a project through a Remote Repository on GitHub. The following topics are covered in this chapter.

TOPICS

1. Git Regular Workflow - Remote Collaboration
2. Remote Collaboration Overview
3. Link With Remote Repository - Git Remote
4. Upload to Remote Repository - Git Push
5. Download Remote Repository and Merge to Local Repository - Git Pull
6. Get Remote Repository Information to Local Repository - Git Fetch
7. Pull vs. Fetch
8. Request for Review and Merge - Pull Request
9. Merge Operation Using GitHub

Git Regular Workflow – Remote Collaboration

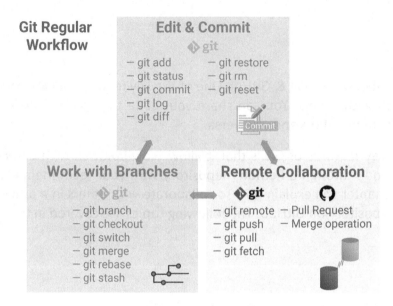

The goal of this chapter is to help you fully understand how to collaborate with others through a Remote Repository on GitHub.

There are two aspects you need to learn about remote collaboration:

1. **Key Git Commands** on your local computer.
2. **GUI (Graphic User Interface) operations** on the GitHub web platform.

1. Key Git commands

In this chapter, we'll cover four key Git commands.

- **git remote**: this command is a multi-use command relating to managing a Remote Repository. For example, with the **git remote add** command, you can establish a link between a Remote Repository and a Local Repository (set up a communication protocol and URL). The **git remote -v** command shows the status of the link.

- **git push**: with this command, you can upload project directories and files along with commit histories for a specified branch from your computer to a Remote Repository

- **git pull**: with this command, you can download project directories and files along with commit histories for a specified branch from a Remote Repository. This command also merges the downloaded branch with an existing branch under the Local Repository.

- **git fetch**: with this command, you can obtain the latest Remote Repository information and store it on your local computer. This command doesn't enforce the merging of the branches in the Local Repository. If you want to update the Local Repository, you need to run the **git merge** or **git checkout** command.

2. GUI operations on the GitHub website

In this chapter, we'll cover two key features of GitHub.

1. **Pull request**: this feature is used for asking a reviewer to review your edits. It is especially helpful when you want to ask the reviewer to merge your branch (a topic branch) with the main (master) branch.

2. **Merge**: this feature gives similar functionality as the **git merge** command and the **git rebase** command. You can execute merge or rebase operations on the GitHub web platform. There are three merge approaches.

   — **Create a merge commit**

   — **Squash and merge**

   — **Rebase and merge**

Remote Collaboration Overview

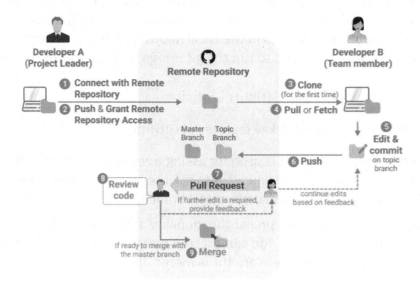

In a typical remote collaboration, you need to seamlessly work on both your local computer (i.e., the command line and a text editor) and a Remote Repository on the GitHub website.

The following is one of the typical flows of remote collaboration on Git & GitHub.

A typical cycle of remote collaboration

1. *Developer A* (a project leader and the owner of the Remote Repository) establishes a link between his Local Repository and the Remote Repository used for the project. To establish the connection, he runs the **git remote** command.

2. Once *Developer A*'s Local Repository is linked with the Remote Repository, he can push his project directory to the Remote Repository by running the **git push** command. He also gives *Developer B* access to the repository at this point.

3. After *Developer B* obtains access to the Remote Repository, she can bring the project directory from the repository by running the **git clone** command. The **git clone** command establishes a link between the Remote Repository and her Local Repository, and the command also creates a copy of the project directory on her local computer.

4. There are two approaches for getting the project files from the Remote Repository the second time:

   1) Running the **git pull** command

   2) Running the **git fetch** command followed by the **git merge** command.

   Note: The **git pull** command works as the **git fetch** command and **git merge** command. The **git pull** command is useful to save time, however, there are some cases when you need to run the **git fetch** command. This will be explained later.

5. Once *Developer B* obtains the project directory under the *master* branch, she is ready to make her edits (e.g., adding a new feature of the program). To start her editing, she creates a new branch (topic branch) to separate her work from the main line of code development. After that, she edits the code on the new branch and creates a commit when her work is done.

6. To share the edited code under the topic branch, *Developer B* pushes the branch into the Remote Repository by running the **git push** command.

7. At this stage, the code edited by *Developer B* is not integrated into the *master* branch yet. Before integrating it, she asks *Developer A* to review the code and merge it with the master branch through a **pull request**. A pull request is a form on GitHub to create a request for a reviewer to review code and merge it with the main branch (e.g., the *master* branch).

8. Once *Developer A* receives a pull request, he reviews the code and decides if the new code is ready to merge or still requires further edits. If further edits are required, he gives *Developer B* feedback on her code.

9. If the code developed by *Developer B* is ready to merge, *Developer A* merges the topic branch with the master branch on the GitHub website.

Practice

Objective:
Prepare for practices

This section gives you information about how to prepare for practice in this chapter. The actual practice will start from the next page.

1. Accounts used in the practice explanation

As explained earlier, to fully understand the remote collaboration approach with Git and GitHub, you need to understand at least two different user perspectives:

1. The owner of the Remote Repository (*Developer A*)
2. A collaborator of the Remote Repository (*Developer B*)

The roles and account information details are described in the illustration below.

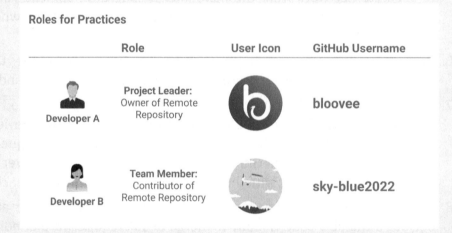

If there are two roles in the practice section on the same page, we'll use the following boxes to make it clear from which perspective the section is being explained.

Action by Developer A

Developer A's actions are described here

---

2. Commit history rules for this practice

For practice purposes, we set a rule for commit messages, so that you can easily follow what each commit is about.

Example

commit message "**M2LB**"

M - Branch (e.g., *M* is *Master*, *A* is *Branch_A*)

2 - Commit order (e.g., *2* is the second commit on the branch)

L - Local vs. Remote (*L* is committed in the Local Repository, *R* is committed in the Remote Repository)

B - Developer who made the commit (e.g., *A* is *Developer A*, *B* is *Developer B*)

We also put the same letters as the content of practice files that are committed so you can easily see the relations between the commit and the edited content.

Note: This approach is only for practice purposes. In actual projects, you need to use a concise description of the key changes in the code (e.g., *"fixed landing page UI"*, *"integrated APIs"*, etc.).

Link With Remote Repository – Git Remote

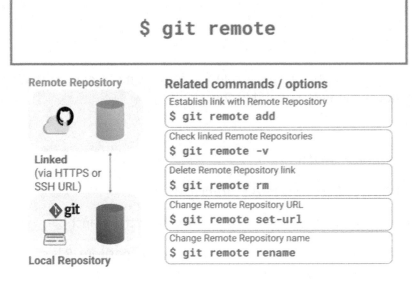

```
$ git remote
```

Remote Repository

Linked
(via HTTPS or
SSH URL)

Local Repository

Related commands / options

Establish link with Remote Repository
```
$ git remote add
```

Check linked Remote Repositories
```
$ git remote -v
```

Delete Remote Repository link
```
$ git remote rm
```

Change Remote Repository URL
```
$ git remote set-url
```

Change Remote Repository name
```
$ git remote rename
```

git remote is the command used when you want to establish and check the linking status between a Remote Repository and your Local Repository. There are some derivative commands and options for this command. We'll explain five major usages in this page.

Key Git Remote Commands

- **git remote add**: Establish a link with a Remote Repository
- **git remote -v**: Check the status of the linked Remote Repository
- **git remote rm**: Delete the Remote Repository link
- **git remote set-url**: Change the Remote Repository URL
- **git remote rename**: Change the Remote Repository name

1. git remote add

Establishes a link between a Local Repository and a Remote Repository. As explained before, when you launch a project as the owner of the Remote Repository, you need to upload your project directory to the Remote Repository first. Before pushing the code, you need to establish a link between your Local Repository and the Remote Repository. The command to establish the link is **git remote add**. You need to specify a Remote Repository name and Remote Repository URL as shown below. The Remote Repository name is typically *origin*. You can get the URL from the Remote Repository page on GitHub.

```
git remote add [Remote Repository name] [Remote Repository URL]
```

2. git remote -v

Checks registered Remote Repositories. After you create a link with a Remote Repository by running the **git remote add** command or the **git clone** command, you may want to check the status of the link. **git remote -v** is the command used to check the status of the Remote Repository linked with your Local Repository. This command doesn't require any argument as shown below.

```
git remote -v
```

3. git remote rm

Deletes the Remote Repository link. When you want to deregister the link in the Remote Repository, the **git remote rm** command is used. To run the command, you need to specify the Remote Repository name as shown below.

```
git remote rm [Remote Repository name]
```

4. git remote set-url

Changes the Remote Repository URL. When you want to change an SSH connection to an HTTPS connection or you simply want to change the URL of the Remote Repository, you can run the **git remote set-url** command. When you run the command, you need to specify the existing Remote Repository name and new URL.

```
git remote set-url [existing Remote Repository name] [new URL]
```

5. git remote rename

Changes the Remote Repository name. The typical name of a Remote Repository is *origin*. However, there may be a situation, such as managing multiple Remote Repositories at the same time, when you want to use different names for the Remote Repositories. You can change the Remote Repository name by running the **git remote rename** command.

> git remote rename [existing Remote Repository name] [new Remote Repository name]

For a better understanding, please go through the following practice section.

Practice

Developer A (Project Owner Role)

Objective:
Check how the git remote commands work

1. Setup a practice project directory and file for this chapter

Directory and file structure

For this practice, we'll use the following directory and file. The directory and file will be used throughout the practices in this chapter.

- Practice project directory: *git_remote_practice*
- Practice file: *git_remote_practice.html*

The screenshot below is the <u>target directory structure</u> example based on Mac OS.

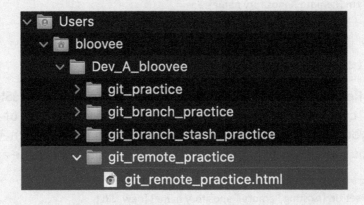

Create the practice project directory and file

Open the project's main directory (e.g., *Dev_A_bloovee*) with VS Code. You can use drag & drop to open the directory.

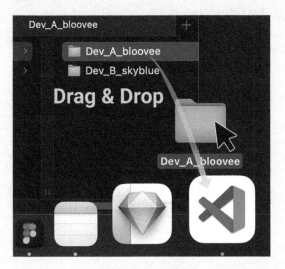

You can also use the command line to move the current directory to the main project directory.

Command Line - INPUT

```
cd ~/Dev_A_bloovee
```

After opening the project's main directory with VS Code, open a new terminal in the VS Code window and run the command below to create the directory and file.

Command Line - INPUT

```
mkdir git_remote_practice
cd git_remote_practice
touch git_remote_practice.html
```

Edit the practice HTML file

For the HTML file, make edits like those shown below. We'll use four branches. For practice purposes, create a coding section for each branch. For the first commit on the master branch, add *<h1>M1LA</h1>* after *<!-- Master Branch-->*.

M1LA indicates the following for practice purposes:

- **M** - Master Branch
- **1** - 1st commit on the branch
- **L** - Committed in the Local Repository
- **A** - Committed by *Developer A*

git_remote_practice.html (master)

```
<!doctype html>
<html lang="en">
<body>
<!-- Master Branch-->
<h1>M1LA</h1>
<!-- /Master Branch-->

<!-- Branch A-->
N/A
<!-- /Branch A-->

<!-- Branch B-->
N/A
<!-- /Branch B-->

<!-- Branch C-->
N/A
<!-- /Branch C-->
</body>
```

Create a Local Repository and make the first commit

As we are working on a new directory, we need to create a new Local Repository. Also, let's make the first commit with the commit message *"M1LA"*, and check the commit status.

Command Line - INPUT

```
git init
git add .
git commit -am "M1LA"
git log --oneline
```

You can see that the first commit was successfully made.

hint: Using 'master' as the name for the initial branch. This default branch name
:
hint: git branch -m <name>
Initialized empty Git repository in /Users/bloovee/Dev_A_bloovee/git_remote_
practice/.git/
[master (root-commit) 4b30a1c] M1LA
  1 file changed, 19 insertions(+)
  create mode 100644 git_remote_practice.html
4b30a1c (HEAD -> master) M1LA

2. Create a Remote Repository

Next, create a new Remote Repository for this practice. Go to the GitHub website and log into your account. Click the **+** button on the top right and select **New repository**. You'll reach the page as shown below. Add the Repository name (use the same name as your project directory (*git_remote_practice*) to avoid confusion.

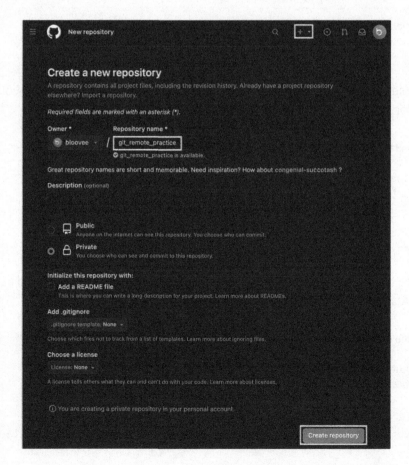

After you press the green button to create a new repository, you'll see the following Quick setup page.

First, we'll try to use the HTTPS connection. Copy the URL by clicking the button on the right.

Go back to the command line and run the **git remote add** command with a Remote Repository name (typically, *origin* is used) and the URL copied from the GitHub website. Also, run the **git remote -v** command to check the Remote Repository status.

Command Line - INPUT (for HTTPS)

```
git remote add origin https://github.com/bloovee/git_remote_practice.git
git remote -v
```

You can see that the Remote Repository was successfully registered in your Local Repository.

Command Line - RESPONSE

```
origin  https://github.com/bloovee/git_remote_practice.git (fetch)
origin  https://github.com/bloovee/git_remote_practice.git (push)
```

3. Delete a Remote Repository link

To delete the Remote Repository link, run the **git remote rm** command as shown below. Also, run the **git remote -v** command to check the status.

Command Line - INPUT

```
git remote rm origin
git remote -v
```

There will be no response as the Remote Repository was already deleted.

For the next step, add the Remote Repository again.

Command Line - INPUT

git remote add origin https://github.com/bloovee/git_remote_practice.git
git remote -v

Confirm that the Remote Repository was correctly registered.

Command Line - RESPONSE

origin https://github.com/bloovee/git_remote_practice.git (fetch)
origin https://github.com/bloovee/git_remote_practice.git (push)

4. Change the Remote Repository URL

In this practice, we try to change the Remote Repository URL from HTTPS to SSH. First, get the new URL from the Remote Repository. Click the SSH button and click the right button to copy the URL.

Run the **git remote set-url** command with the copied URL. Also, run the **git remote -v** command to confirm the status.

Command Line - INPUT (for SSH)

git remote set-url origin git@github.com:bloovee/git_remote_practice.git
git remote -v

You can see that the URL changed to SSH URL.

Command Line - RESPONSE

origin git@github.com:bloovee/git_remote_practice.git (fetch)
origin git@github.com:bloovee/git_remote_practice.git (push)

5. Change the Remote Repository name

Lastly, try to change the Remote Repository name. This time change the name from *origin* to *origin_2* as shown below.

Command Line - INPUT

```
git remote rename origin origin_2
git remote -v
```

You can see that the name has changed to *origin_2*.

Command Line - RESPONSE

```
origin_2 git@github.com:bloovee/git_remote_practice.git (fetch)
origin_2 git@github.com:bloovee/git_remote_practice.git (push)
```

For the next practice, revert the name to *origin*.

Command Line - INPUT

```
git remote rename origin_2 origin
git remote -v
```

Confirm the name was changed back to *origin*.

Command Line - RESPONSE

```
origin git@github.com:bloovee/git_remote_practice.git (fetch)
origin git@github.com:bloovee/git_remote_practice.git (push)
```

Upload to Remote Repository – Git Push

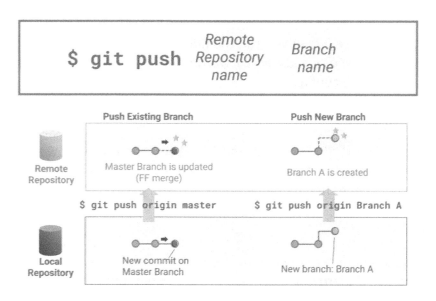

Push is used when you want changes made to the Local Repository to be reflected in the Remote Repository. After establishing the link between the Remote Repository and the Local Repository using the **git remote add** command or the **git clone** command, you can upload your changes into the linked Remote Repository by running the **git push** command.

When you push a branch, you need to specify the branch name after the Remote Repository name. Typically, **origin** is used for a Remote Repository name. The following is an example of pushing the *master* branch to the Remote Repository.

```
git push origin master
```

Push Operation

Mainly, there are two cases in the push operation.

1. Push an existing branch

This is the case when the branch exists in both the Local Repository and the Remote Repository. In this case, when you run the push command, the branch is uploaded to the Remote Repository, and **Fast-Forward merge** is triggered unless the pushed branch doesn't create conflicts.

2. Push a new branch

This is the case when the branch is created in the Local Repository; however, it doesn't exist in the Remote Repository. In this case, when you run the push command, the pushed branch is generated in the Remote Repository.

Conflicts

When you push a branch to the Remote Repository, Git checks if the pushed branch creates a conflict. If there is any conflict, the push operation is terminated.

You'll see an error message like the one below when you encounter a conflict.

git_remote_practice.html (master)

```
To https://github.com/bloovee/git_remote_practice.git
 ! [rejected]        master -> master (fetch first)
error: failed to push some refs to '
https://github.com/bloovee/git_remote_practice.git'
hint: Updates were rejected because the remote contains work that you do not
hint: have locally. This is usually caused by another repository pushing to
hint: the same ref. If you want to integrate the remote changes, use
hint: 'git pull' before pushing again.
hint: See the 'Note about fast-forwards' in 'git push --help' for details.
```

For example, you'll face a conflict when an advanced commit already exists on the same branch in the Remote Repository like in *Case A* in the illustration below: commit *M3R* already exists in the Remote Repository while commit *M3L* in the Local Repository is being pushed.

When you are pushing the code to a new branch, it is safer. It will be like *Case B* in the illustration below: commit *A1* in *Branch A* (new branch) doesn't conflict with commit *M3R* in the *master* branch unless you trigger the merge operation.

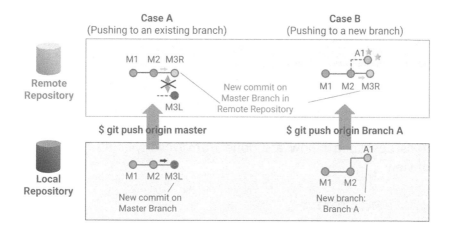

The -u option

In a typical Git operation, the **git push** command is often used to upload edited files on the same branch in the same Remote Repository. To avoid typing a Remote Repository name and a branch name every time, you can use the **-u** option or **-set-upstream** option (the meaning of upstream will be explained on the **git fetch** page). After running the command with the **-u** option, you don't need to specify a Remote Repository name and a branch name again.

For the first push command, run:

```
git push -u origin master
```

After the first command (no need to type **origin** and *master* anymore), run:

```
git push
```

After the push operation

When you push your code to the Remote Repository, other developers who have access to the Remote Repository (collaborators) can see it on the GitHub web platform and download it to their local computer by the **git pull** or **git fetch** command. You can also ask one of the collaborators to review and merge their code with a main branch (e.g., *master* branch) by triggering a **pull request**.

For a better understanding, please go through the following practice section.

Practice

Objective:
Learn how to push branches

All actions described below are done from *Developer A's* (project owner's) point of view

1. Prepare a practice file

Use the same file as in the previous practice on the previous page (the **git remote** page). We already made one commit on the *master* branch. If you haven't created the file, go back to the previous page.

2. Push a file to an existing branch

As the URL of the Remote Repository is already registered, you are ready to run the push command.

Command Line - INPUT

```
git push origin master
```

When you run the command, the command line may ask you to type in your password depending on the SSH or HTTPS settings. For HTTPS connection, you need to use PAT (Personal Access Token).

Command Line - RESPONSE

```
Enumerating objects: 5, done.
:
To https://github.com/bloovee/git_remote_practice.git
* [new branch] master -> master
```

Go to the Remote Repository on the GitHub website. After refreshing the browser, you can see that the project directory git_remote_practice is successfully uploaded to the Remote Repository as shown below.

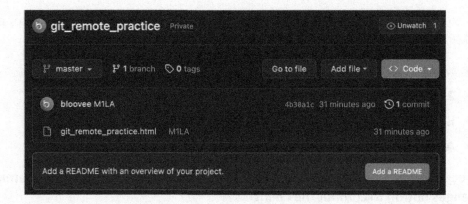

3. Create conflicted commits on the Local and Remote Repositories

This section is just for practice purposes. We'll explain under what conditions you cannot execute the push command.

Edit the file on the Remote Repository

First, make a new commit directly on the Remote Repository.

In the Remote Repository, select the *git_remote_practice.html* file

You can see the content of the HTML file as shown below. Press the **pen icon** on the right to edit the file.

Edit the file like below (adding *<h1>M2RA</h1>*).

git_remote_practice.html (master)

```
<!-- Master Branch-->
<h1>M1LA</h1>
<h1>M2RA</h1>
<!-- /Master Branch-->
```

Go to the bottom of the site and add a commit message. In this practice, put "*M2RA*". *M2RA* indicates the following for practice purposes;

- **M** - Master branch
- **2** - 2nd commit on the branch
- **R** - Committed in the Remote Repository
- **A** - Committed by *Developer A*

Select "**commit directly to the master branch**" and click the green **Commit changes** button to commit the change.

Edit the file on the local computer

Now, go back to the editor on your local computer and edit like shown below (the same edit as the one on the Remote Repository).

git_remote_practice.html (master)

```
<!-- Master Branch-->
<h1>M1LA</h1>
<h1>M2LA</h1>
<!-- /Master Branch-->
```

Commit the change with the commit message of *"M2LA"*. *M2LA* indicates the following for practice purposes:

- **M** - Master branch
- **2** - 2nd commit on the branch
- **L** - Committed in the Local Repository
- **A** - Committed by *Developer A*

And run the **git log** command.

Command Line - INPUT

```
git commit -am "M2LA"
git log --oneline
```

You can see the commit history like shown below.

Command Line - RESPONSE

```
77e4ddf (HEAD -> master) M2LA
4b30a1c (origin/master) M1LA
```

The current situation is similar to Case A explained at the beginning of this page.

Run the **git push** command to see the result.

Command Line - INPUT

```
git push origin master
```

As there is commit *M2RA* in the Remote Repository already, the push command is rejected.

To https://github.com/bloovee/git_remote_practice.git
 ! [rejected] master -> master (fetch first)
error: failed to push some refs to
'https://github.com/bloovee/git_remote_practice.git'
hint: Updates were rejected because the remote contains work that you do not
hint: have locally. This is usually caused by another repository pushing to
hint: the same ref. If you want to integrate the remote changes, use
hint: 'git pull' before pushing again.
hint: See the 'Note about fast-forwards' in 'git push --help' for details.

4. Push a file to a new branch

As we cannot push the change to the *master* branch, create a new branch *Branch_A* and checkout to the branch. To confirm the commit history on the branch, also run the **git log** command.

Command Line - INPUT

```
git checkout -b Branch_A
git log --oneline
```

You can see that the status of *Branch_A* is the same as the status of the *master* branch.

Command Line - RESPONSE

Switched to a new branch 'Branch_A'
77e4ddf (HEAD -> Branch_A, master) M2LA
4b30a1c (origin/master) M1LA

Currently, *Branch_A* doesn't exist in the Remote Repository. Push *Branch_A* to see the result.

Command Line - INPUT

```
git push origin Branch_A
```

You can see that *Branch_A* was successfully pushed to the Remote Repository although the code of the *master* branch and *Branch_A* are the same. This is because you can avoid clashing code on the same branch and give room to reconcile on the Remote Repository later.

Command Line - RESPONSE

```
Enumerating objects: 6, done.
Counting objects: 100% (6/6), done.
Delta compression using up to 10 threads
Compressing objects: 100% (6/6), done.
Writing objects: 100% (6/6), 561 bytes | 561.00 KiB/s, done.
Total 6 (delta 1), reused 0 (delta 0), pack-reused 0
remote: Resolving deltas: 100% (1/1), done.
remote:
remote: Create a pull request for 'Branch_A' on GitHub by visiting:
remote: https://github.com/bloovee/git_remote_practice/pull/new/Branch_A
remote:
To https://github.com/bloovee/git_remote_practice.git
* [new branch] Branch_A -> Branch_A
```

Go to the Remote Repository on the GitHub website; exit the code browsing mode by clicking the *git_remote_practice* repository. You can confirm that *Branch_A* was created in the browser as shown below.

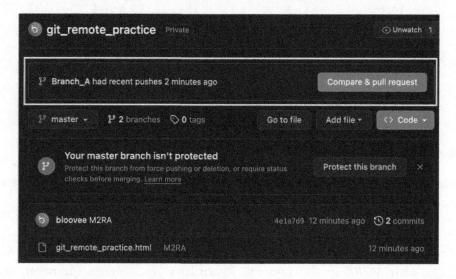

5. Clean up the master branch conflict

As we intentionally created conflicting commits - commit *M2LA* and *M2RA* in the Local Repository and the Remote Repository - let's clean them up before going to the next practice.

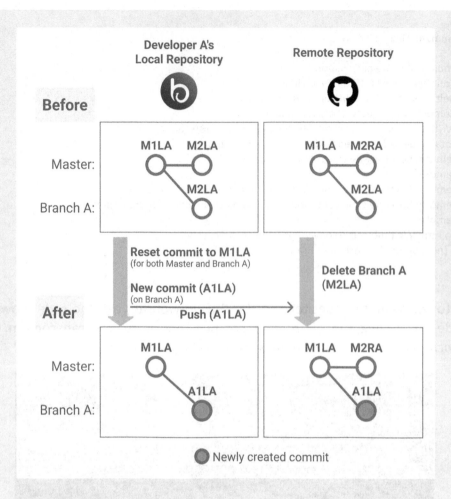

Developer A's Local Repository

Remote Repository

Before

Master: M1LA M2LA

Branch A: M2LA

Master: M1LA M2RA

Branch A: M2LA

Reset commit to M1LA
(for both Master and Branch A)

New commit (A1LA)
(on Branch A)

Push (A1LA)

Delete Branch A
(M2LA)

After

Master: M1LA

Branch A: A1LA

Master: M1LA M2RA

Branch A: A1LA

● Newly created commit

First, clean up Branch_A

Currently, *Branch_A* and the *master* branch are the same. We want to create a unique code for *Branch_A* for practice purposes.

Reset commit histories to commit *M1LA* on *Branch_A*. This is for recreating *Branch_A* from the first commit of the *master* branch because commit *M2LA* conflicts with *M2RA* in the Remote Repository. To execute **git reset**, use a Commit Hash generated on your computer for commit *M1LA*.

Command Line - INPUT

```
git reset --hard 4b30a1c
```

You can see that the *HEAD* is back to *M1LA*.

```
HEAD is now at 4b30a1c M1LA
```

Now create a correct version of *Branch_A*. Edit the HTML file like below (adding *<h1>A1LA</h1>* after *<!-- Branch A-->*.

A1LA indicates the following for practice purposes:

- **A** - Branch_A
- **1** - 1st commit on the branch
- **L** - Committed in the Local branch
- **A** - Committed by *Developer A*

git_remote_practice.html (Branch_A)

```
<!-- Master Branch-->
<h1>M1LA</h1>
<!-- /Master Branch-->

<!-- Branch A-->
<h1>A1LA</h1>
<!-- /Branch A-->
```

Commit the change with the commit message of *"A1LA"* and check the log.

Command Line - INPUT

```
git commit -am "A1LA"
git log --oneline
```

You can see that the *HEAD* of *Branch_A* is now *A1LA* and it has diverged from the *master* branch at commit *M1LA*.

Command Line - RESPONSE

```
545ffbb (HEAD -> Branch_A) A1LA
4b30a1c (origin/master) M1LA
```

As *Branch_A* on the Remote Repository is still in its old status, go to the Remote Repository and delete it to avoid a conflict. This is for practice purposes. You need to carefully manage the process when deleting a branch on the Remote Repository.

To delete a branch, press the **branch selection pull-down** on the left and click **View all branches**.

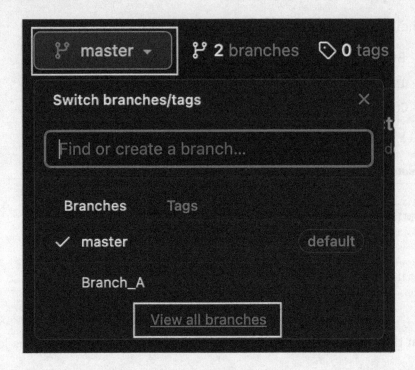

Click the delete button on *Branch_A* as shown below.

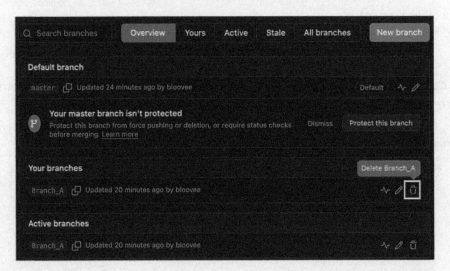

You can see that *Branch_A* was successfully deleted:

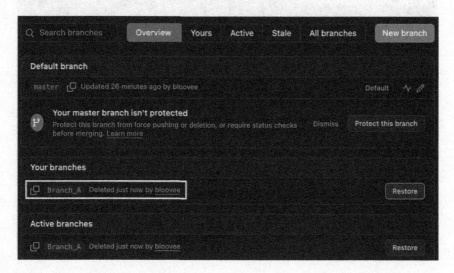

To update *Branch_A* on the Remote Repository, push *Branch_A*.

Command Line - INPUT

```
git push origin Branch_A
```

You can see that *Branch_A* was pushed successfully.

Command Line - RESPONSE

```
Enumerating objects: 6, done.
:
* [new branch] Branch_A -> Branch_A
```

You can also confirm that the latest commit is *A1LA* on the Remote Repository as shown in the image below.

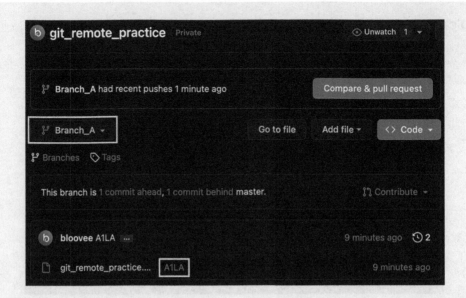

Next, clean up the master branch

Switch the current branch to the *master* branch and check the log.

Command Line - INPUT

```
git checkout master
git log --oneline
```

You can see that *M2LA*, which conflicts with the commit on the Remote Repository, is still the *HEAD* of the *master* branch as we reset it only on *Branch_A*.

Command Line - RESPONSE

```
77e4ddf (HEAD -> master) M2LA
4b30a1c (origin/master) M1LA
```

Reset the *master* branch to commit *M1LA*. Use the Commit Hash generated on your computer for commit *M1LA*.

Command Line - INPUT

```
git reset --hard 4b30a1c
```

You can see that the *HEAD* of the *master* branch is now back to *M1LA*.

Command Line - RESPONSE

```
HEAD is now at 4b30a1c M1LA
```

Download Remote Repository and Merge to Local Repository – Git Pull

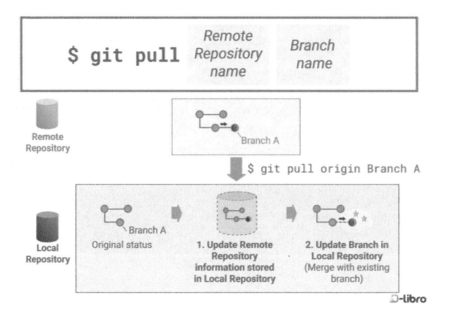

$-Libro

Pull is used when you want to download the latest Remote Repository information and merge it with the existing branch in the Local Repository. **git pull** is the command used to execute the pull action. The **git pull** command is often explained as a shortcut command for **git fetch** and **git merge**. As the **git pull** command shortcuts the manual checking process of the Remote Repository information, it may create a conflict. For a simple operation, you can use the pull command. However, generally, it is safer to use the **git fetch** command and check the Remote Repository status first before executing the **git merge** command.

For a better understanding, please go through the following practice section.

Practice

Objective:

Check how the pull operation works from both the repository owner and collaborator's points of view

In this practice, we'll use the following two users: *Developer A* and *Developer B*.

1. Download the project files for the first time: $ git clone

This is the same step we explained in Chapter 3. As we are using a different repository, you need to go through the same process again.

Action by Developer A

Before Developer B accesses the Remote Repository, Developer A needs to grant access to it.

Go to Settings of the repository and select Manage access. Press the green button to add a collaborator.

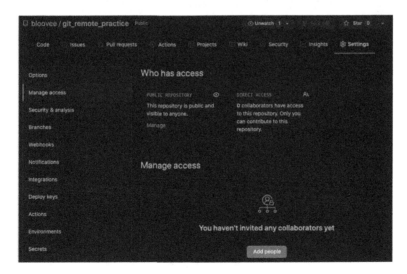

Find a collaborator. In this demo, we invite **sky-blue2022 (Developer B)**.

Next, we'll be explaining the steps from *Developer B*'s point of view.

Action by Developer B

After *Developer A* sends an invitation, Developer B receives an email with the invitation like shown below.

@bloovee has invited you to collaborate on the
bloovee/git_remote_practice repository

You can accept or decline this invitation. You can also visit @bloovee to learn a bit more about them.

This invitation will expire in 7 days.

Note: This invitation was intended for connectthesky2022@gmail.com. If you were not expecting this invitation, you can ignore this email. If @bloovee is sending you too many emails, you can block them or report abuse.

Click **View invitation** and press the **Access invitation** button like in the image below.

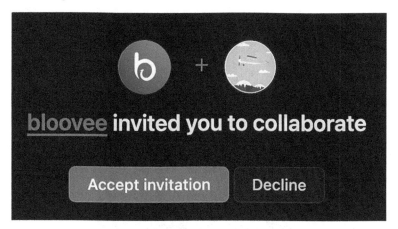

Now you as *Developer B* have access to the Remote Repository. To clone the project file, click the **Code** button and copy the URL for HTTPS.

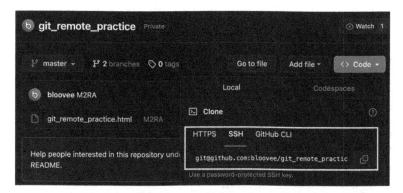

Go to the command line and run the **git clone** command.

Open the main project directory

When you run the **git clone** command., make sure that the current directory is where you want to create the project directory. In this project, you need to set the project's main directory for *Developer B* (e.g., *Dev_B_skyblue*) as the current working directory.

A quick way to open the directory with VS Code is by using drag & drop.

Open a new terminal. You can see that the project's main directory is shown in the *EXPLORER* section on the left and the directory is shown as the current working directory in the terminal.

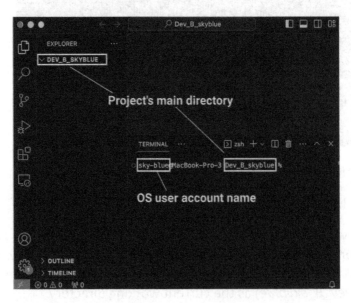

You can also use the command line to move the current directory to the main project directory.

Command Line - INPUT

```
cd ~/Dev_B_skyblue
```

Once you set the current working directory properly, run the command below.

Command Line - INPUT (for SSH)

```
git clone git@github.com:bloovee/git_remote_practice.git
```

or

Command Line - INPUT (for HTTPS

```
git clone https://github.com/bloovee/git_remote_practice.git
```

If the command successfully goes through as shown below, you'll see that the *git_remote_practice* directory is generated under the directory in which you executed the clone command.

Command Line - RESPONSE

```
Cloning into 'git_remote_practice'...
:
Resolving deltas: 100% (2/2), done.
```

2. Run the git pull command

At this stage, the *HEAD* of the *master* branch in each repository is the following.

- *Developer A*'s Local Repository: *M1LA*
- Remote Repository: *M2RA*
- *Developer B*'s Local Repository: *M2RA*

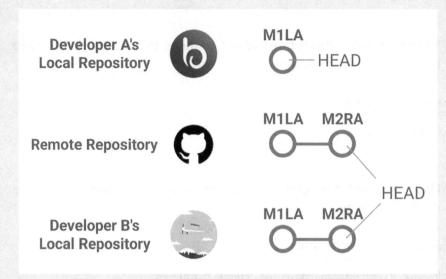

From *Developer B*'s point of view, at this stage, the statuses of the Remote Repository and the Local Repository on the master branch are the same; the *HEAD* is commit *M2RA*. This means that there is nothing you can pull on the *master* branch. However, *Developer A*'s *master* branch lags behind.

To practice the pull command, we'll do the following actions:

1. Pull the *master* branch on *Developer A*'s local computer
2. Further edit the *master* branch on *Developer A*'s computer and push it to the Remote Repository
3. Pull the updated *master* branch on *Developer B*'s local computer

---

Action by Developer A

Run the pull command specifying the Remote Repository name (*origin*) and the *master* branch.

Command Line - INPUT

```
git pull origin master
```

You can see that the *master* branch was updated by the **Fast-forward** merge.

```
bloovee@MBP git_remote_practice % git pull origin master
remote: Enumerating objects: 5, done.
:
Fast-forward
git_remote_practice.html | 3 ++-
  1 file changed, 2 insertions(+), 1 deletion(-)
```

To confirm the commit status, check the log.

Command Line - INPUT

```
git log --oneline
```

You can see that the *HEAD* of the *master* branch in *Developer A*'s Local Repository is the same as the Remote Repository's.

Command Line - RESPONSE

```
4e1a7d9 (HEAD -> master, origin/master) M2RA
4b30a1c M1LA
```

Next, edit the html file on the *master* branch.

git_remote_practice.html (master)

```
<!-- Master Branch-->
<h1>M1LA</h1>
<h1>M2RA</h1>
<h1>M3LA</h1>
<!-- /Master Branch-->
```

Commit the change with the commit message of "*M3LA*" and check the log to see the latest status.

M3LA indicates the following :

- **M** - Master Branch
- **3** - 3rd commit on the branch
- **L** - Committed in the Local Repository
- **A** - Committed by *Developer A*

Command Line - INPUT

```
git commit -am "M3LA"
git log --oneline
```

You can see that a new commit was successfully created as shown below.

Command Line - RESPONSE

```
4e7dbf9 (HEAD -> master) M3LA
4e1a7d9 (origin/master) M2RA
4b30a1c M1LA
```

Finally, push the *master* branch to the Remote Repository.

Command Line - INPUT

```
git push origin master
```

You can see that the latest commit was successfully pushed like shown below.

Command Line - RESPONSE

```
Enumerating objects: 5, done.
   :
To https://github.com/bloovee/git_remote_practice.git
    4e1a7d9..4e7dbf9 master -> master
```

Next, we'll be explaining the steps from *Developer B*'s point of view.

Action by Developer B

Before running the pull command, let's check the commit status.

Command Line - INPUT

```
cd git_remote_practice
git log --oneline
```

You can see only two commits at this stage.

Command Line - RESPONSE

```
4e1a7d9 (HEAD -> master, origin/master, origin/HEAD) M2RA
4b30a1c M1LA
```

To bring the latest commit made by *Developer A* to *Developer B*'s Local Repository, run the pull command.

Command Line - INPUT

```
git pull origin master
```

You can see that Fast-forward merge was executed.

Command Line - RESPONSE

```
remote: Enumerating objects: 5, done.
   :
From github.com:bloovee/git_remote_practice
    * branch master -> FETCH_HEAD
      4e1a7d9..4e7dbf9 master -> origin/master
Updating 4e1a7d9..4e7dbf9
Fast-forward
git_remote_practice.html | 1 +
  1 file changed, 1 insertion(+)
```

Check the commit status again.

Command Line - INPUT

git log --oneline

You can see that commit M3LA made by Developer A was merged with Developer B's master branch.

Command Line - RESPONSE

4e7dbf9 (HEAD -> master, origin/master, origin/HEAD) M3LA
4e1a7d9 M2RA
4b30a1c M1LA

3. Recap of this practice page

To review the summary of what we have done, you can check the illustration below.

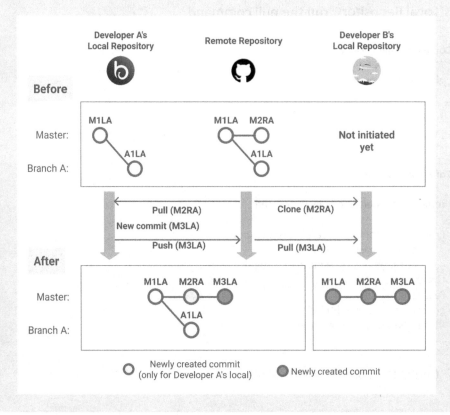

Get Remote Repository Information to Local Repository – Git Fetch

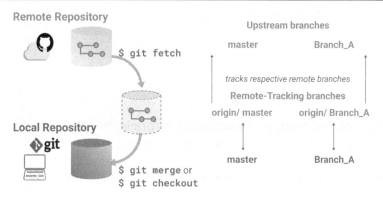

```
$ git fetch Remote Repository name
```

Remote Repository

$ git fetch

Upstream branches

master   Branch_A

tracks respective remote branches

Remote-Tracking branches

origin/ master   origin/ Branch_A

Local Repository

$ git merge or
$ git checkout

master   Branch_A

◯-libro

Fetch is used when you want to get the latest status of the Remote Repository. The command used to execute Fetch is **git fetch**. The command doesn't require a branch name. You'll get the information for all branches under the Remote Repository. To check the Remote Repository branch status, run the **git branch -a** command. The command with the **-a** option shows the status of the remote-tracking branches, which track the upstream branches from the local computer.

There are two major use cases for **git fetch**. The first use case is more important than the second one as the second one can be managed by using the **git pull** command.

1. Bringing a new branch from the Remote Repository

As explained on the previous page, the **git pull** command doesn't work for a new branch. The **git fetch** command is useful when a new branch is created in a Remote Repository and you need to bring it to your Local Repository. The typical command execution process is as follows.

First, run the fetch command to get the Remote Repository data. Then, check the branch name you want to get.

```
git fetch origin
git branch -a
```

You'll see several branch names with different colors like the example below.

Command Line - RESPONSE

```
*   [Current Branch Name]
    [Local Branch Name]
    remotes/origin/[Branch Name]
    remotes/origin/HEAD -> origin/master
    remotes/origin/master
```

- Green: The current local branch
- Black: Local branches
- Red: Remote branch information. remote/origin/HEAD defines the branch that will be checked out when you clone the repository

Finally, switch to the new branch from the remote repository by running the **git checkout** or **git switch** command.

```
git checkout [Branch Name in the Remote Repository]
```

2. Updating an existing branch with the latest status of the Remote Repository

You can use the **git pull** command to update an existing branch, however, if you are not sure about the branch status in the Remote Repository, you can run the **git fetch** command first followed by the **git merge** command as shown below.

First, run the fetch command to get the Remote Repository data.

```
git fetch origin
```

Then, run the merge command from the branch you want to update. For the argument, add **origin/** before the branch name you want to update.

```
git merge origin/[Local Repository name]
```

Note: remote-tracking branch and upstream branch

To have a better understanding of the role of Fetch, understanding the two concepts may be helpful: a remote-tracking branch and an upstream branch. If you are new to Git, you can skip this section. You can come back here when you have built a basic understanding of Git.

- **Remote-tracking branch:** the branch tracks a Remote Repository from the Local Repository (e.g., *origin/master*, *origin/Branch_A*)
- **Upstream branch:** the Remote Repository is tracked by a remote-tracking branch

The following explanation provided in the official Git documentation may give you a better idea about the remote-tracking branch.

"Remote-tracking branches are references to the state of remote branches. They're local references that you can't move; Git moves them for you whenever you do any network communication, to make sure they accurately represent the state of the Remote Repository. Think of them as bookmarks, to remind you where the branches in your remote repositories were the last time you connected to them.

Remote-tracking branch names take the form <remote>/<branch>. For instance, if you wanted to see what the master branch on your origin remote looked like as of the last time you communicated with it, you would check the origin/master branch. If you were working on an issue with a partner and they pushed up an iss53 branch, you might have your own local iss53 branch, but the branch on the server would be represented by the remote-tracking branch origin/iss53."

For a better understanding, please go through the following practice section.

Practice

Objective:
Check how the git fetch command works

1. Check the limitation of the pull command

In this part, we'll explain the steps to do this from the point of view of *Developer B*.

Action by Developer B

First, check the current branch status by running the **git branch** command.

Command Line - INPUT

```
git branch
```

You can see only the master branch on the *Developer B*'s local computer.

Command Line - RESPONSE

```
* master
```

Next, check the branch status of the Remote Repository with the **-a** option. With the option, the **git branch** command shows information including the status of the Remote Repository captured in the Local Repository.

Command Line - INPUT

```
git branch -a
```

Now you can see that *Branch_A* also exists in the Remote Repository. *Branch_A* was created and pushed in the practice section on the git push page.

Command Line - RESPONSE

```
* master
  remotes/origin/Branch_A
  remotes/origin/HEAD -> origin/master
  remotes/origin/master
```

To try to get *Branch_A* in the Local Repository, run the git pull command like shown below.

Command Line - INPUT

```
git pull origin Branch_A
```

You will see a message like the one below. (You may see different messages if you are using Windows. We'll explain that later.)

Command Line - RESPONSE

```
From github.com:bloovee/git_remote_practice
 * branch Branch_A -> FETCH_HEAD
hint: You have divergent branches and need to specify how to reconcile them.
hint: You can do so by running one of the following commands sometime before
hint: your next pull:
hint:
hint: git config pull.rebase false # merge
hint: git config pull.rebase true # rebase
hint: git config pull.ff only # fast-forward only
hint:
hint: You can replace "git config" with "git config --global" to set a default
hint: preference for all repositories. You can also pass --rebase, --no-rebase,
hint: or --ff-only on the command line to override the configured default per
hint: invocation.
fatal: Need to specify how to reconcile divergent branches.
```

To confirm the latest branch status, run the **git branch** command again.

Command Line - INPUT

```
git branch
```

You can see only the master branch. This means that the **git pull** command doesn't work for a new branch that doesn't exist in the Local Repository yet.

```
* master
```

For Windows (Git Bash)

For Windows, the result of the **git pull** command can be different. You may see an auto-merging action after running the **git pull** command.

```
From github.com:bloovee/git_remote_practice
 * branch            Branch_A -> FETCH_HEAD
Auto-merging git_remote_practice.html
Merge made by the 'ort' strategy.
 git_remote_practice.html | 2 +-
 1 file changed, 1 insertion(+), 1 deletion(-)
```

Because of this, the *master* branch commit history changes. You can confirm the status by running the **git log** command.

```
git log --oneline --graph
```

```
* 4b38e3e (HEAD -> master) Merge branch 'Branch_A' of github.com:bloovee/
git_remote_practice3
|\
| * 545ffbb (origin/Branch_A) A1LA
* | 4e7dbf9 (origin/master, origin/HEAD) M3LA
* | 4e1a7d9 M2RA
|/
* 4b30a1c M1LA
```

Before going to the next step, reset to the commit *M3LA*.

Command Line - INPUT

```
git reset --hard 4e7dbf9
git log --oneline --graph
```

Command Line - RESPONSE

```
* 4e7dbf9 (HEAD -> master, origin/master, origin/HEAD) M3LA
* 4e1a7d9 M2RA
* 4b30a1c M1LA
```

2. Bring a new branch to the Local Repository — after the pull command execution

In this part, we'll explain the steps to do this from the point of view of *Developer B*.

Action by Developer B

As the **git pull** command executes the **git fetch** command first, all branch information in the Remote Repository is brought to the Local Repository. We already confirmed it by running the **git branch -a** command. To bring a branch that already exists in the Remote Repository to the Local Repository, you need to simply run either the **git checkout** or **git switch** command. Try the command and check the branch status.

Command Line - INPUT

```
git checkout Branch_A
git branch
```

Branch_A is registered under the Local Repository and it becomes the current branch.

3. Test the fetch command

As we executed the **git pull** command first, the functionality of the **git fetch** command is still not clearly explained. For a better understanding, create another branch on the repository owner's side (*Developer A*).

Action by Developer A

Create a new branch, *Branch_B,* and switch to the branch by running the following command.

Command Line - INPUT

```
git checkout -b Branch_B
```

You can confirm that the current branch is switched to the new branch, *Branch_B*.

Command Line - RESPONSE

```
Switched to a new branch 'Branch_B'
```

Edit the html file as shown below (add code after *<!-- Branch B-->*). *B1LA* indicates the following for a practice purpose:

- **B** - Branch_B
- **1** - 1st commit on the branch
- **L** - Committed in the Local Repository
- **A** - Committed by *Developer A*.

Switched to a new branch 'Branch_B'

```
<!-- Branch B-->
<h1>B1LA</h1>
<!-- /Branch B-->
```

Commit the change and check the log.

Command Line - INPUT

```
git commit -am "B1LA"
git log --oneline
```

You can confirm that a new commit was made on *Branch_B*.

Command Line - RESPONSE

```
92ea341 (HEAD -> Branch_B) B1LA
4e7dbf9 (origin/master, master) M3LA
4e1a7d9 M2RA
4b30a1c M1LA
```

Push the new branch, *Branch_B*.

Command Line - INPUT

```
git push origin Branch_B
```

You can confirm that the new *Branch_B* was pushed to the Remote Repository.

Command Line - RESPONSE

```
Enumerating objects: 5, done.
:
* [new branch] Branch_B -> Branch_B
```

Let's also update *Branch_A* to do another test. Switch to *Branch_A*.

Command Line - INPUT

```
git checkout Branch_A
```

Command Line - RESPONSE

```
Switched to branch 'Branch_A'
```

Edit the file as shown below (Add *A2LA*). *A2LA* indicates the following for practice purposes:

- **A** - Branch_A
- **2** - 2nd commit on the branch
- **L** - Committed in the Local Repository
- **A** - Committed by *Developer A*

git_remote_practice.html (Branch_A)

```
<!-- Branch A-->
<h1>A1LA</h1>
<h1>A2LA</h1>
<!-- /Branch A-->
```

Then, commit the change and check the log.

Command Line - INPUT

```
git commit -am "A2LA"
git log --oneline
```

Command Line - RESPONSE

```
2c7c0e7 (HEAD -> Branch_A) A2LA
545ffbb (origin/Branch_A) A1LA
4b30a1c M1LA
```

Push the branch to the Remote Repository.

Command Line - INPUT

Command Line - INPUT

git push origin Branch_A

Command Line - RESPONSE

Enumerating objects: 5, done.

:

    545ffbb..2c7c0e7 Branch_A -> Branch_A

Next, we'll try to bring the new commit to *Developer B*'s Local Repository by running the **git fetch** command.

Action by Developer B

To check the Remote Repository status in *Developer B*'s Local Repository, run the **git branch -a** command.

Command Line - INPUT

git branch -a

You can see that there is <u>no information about *Branch_B*.</u>

Command Line - RESPONSE

* Branch_A
  master
  remotes/origin/Branch_A
  remotes/origin/HEAD -> origin/master
  remotes/origin/master

Fetch the remote repository

Run the **git fetch** command to update the Remote Repository information.

```
git fetch
```

You can see that there are two updates

1. *Branch_A* is updated
2. New branch *Branch_B* is created

```
remote: Enumerating objects: 10, done.
:
From github.com:bloovee/git_remote_practice
545ffbb..2c7c0e7 Branch_A -> origin/Branch_A
* [new branch]     Branch_B            -> origin/Branch_B
```

Run the **git branch -a** command again to see the latest branch status.

```
git branch -a
```

You can see that *Branch_B* is under the Remote Repository, however, it is still not in the Local Repository.

```
* Branch_A
  master
  remotes/origin/Branch_A
  remotes/origin/Branch_B
  remotes/origin/HEAD -> origin/master
  remotes/origin/master
```

Checkout Branch_B

To bring it to the Local Repository, run either the **git checkout** or **git switch** command as shown below.

```
git checkout Branch_B
```

You can see that the current branch was switched to *Branch_B*.

```
branch 'Branch_B' set up to track 'origin/Branch_B'.
Switched to a new branch 'Branch_B'
```

Checkout and merge Branch_A

You also need to update *Branch_A*. Switch to *Branch_A*.

```
git checkout Branch_A
```

You can see a message saying *Branch_A* is behind *Branch_A* in the Remote Repository.

```
Switched to branch 'Branch_A'
Your branch is behind 'origin/Branch_A' by 1 commit, and can be fast-forwarded.
(use "git pull" to update your local branch)
```

To update *Branch_A*, you can run either the **git pull** command or the **git merge** command. For practice purposes, we use the **git merge** command here. Use *origin/Branch_A* as the argument of the command.

Command Line - INPUT

```
git merge origin/Branch_A
```

You can see that the Fast-forward merge was executed.

Command Line - RESPONSE

```
Updating 545ffbb..2c7c0e7
Fast-forward
 git_remote_practice.html | 3 ++-
 1 file changed, 2 insertions(+), 1 deletion(-)
```

Check the log.

Command Line - INPUT

```
git log --oneline
```

Command Line - RESPONSE

```
2c7c0e7 (HEAD, origin/Branch_A, Branch_A) A2LA
545ffbb A1LA
4b30a1c M1LA
```

5. Checking the branch status

Now all repositories (*Developer A*'s Local Repository, *Developer B*'s Local Repository, and the Remote Repository) have the same status.

To see the status of the Remote Repository, go to the repository on the GitHub website. Select *Branch_B* on the branch selection pull-down on the left and click the **clock button** on the right.

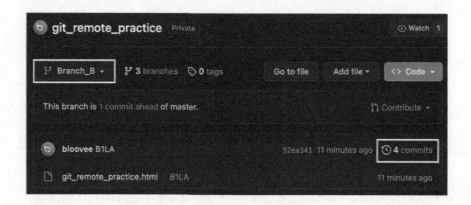

You can see the commit history of *Branch_B* in the Remote Repository.

For the Local Repository, run the **git log** command for each branch for each user.

The illustration below is the summary of the latest statuses.

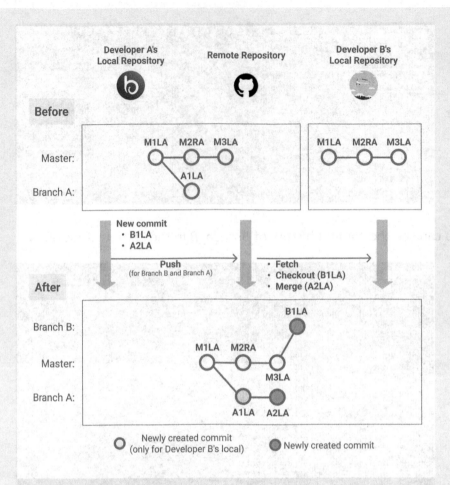

Pull vs. Fetch

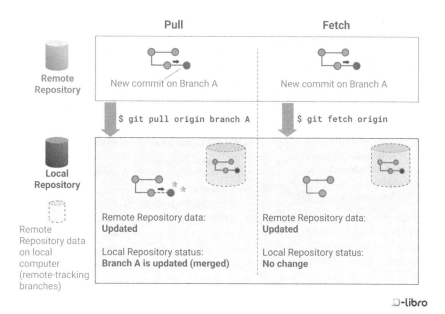

This page compares **Pull** with **Fetch**.

The key difference between Pull (the **git pull** command) and Fetch (the **git fetch** command) is whether the command executes the merge action or not.

Both commands download commits and files from a Remote Repository under remote-tracking branches (the Remote Repository information). The pull command

seamlessly triggers the merge action for the designated branch, while the fetch command doesn't initiate the merge action.

Typically, the pull command is used for the efficiency of operations. For a simple operation, you can use the pull command. However, generally, it is safer to use the **git fetch** command and check the Remote Repository status first before executing the **git merge** command.

Request for Review and Merge – Pull Request

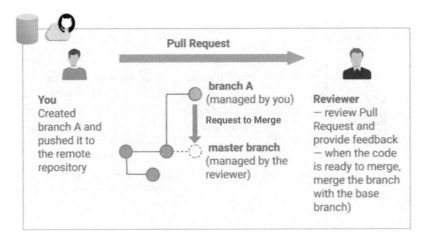

Pull Request in GitHub is used to create a request to review changes made on a topic branch and merge it with a main branch (e.g., the master branch). It has nothing to do with the pull command although the naming is similar. To avoid confusion, you can memorize it as a merge request. In GitLab, it is in fact called a ***merge request***.

Before triggering a pull request, you need to push an edited branch to a Remote Repository. After pushing the branch, you can ask a reviewer to review and merge with the main branch. You can initiate a pull request on the GitHub website.

For a better understanding, please go through the following practice section.

Practice

Learn how the Pull Request operation works

The scenario of this practice is the following

1. *Developer B* works on creating a new feature on a new branch *Branch_C*, and pushes the code to the Remote Repository

2. *Developer B* triggers a **pull request** to ask *Developer A* to review and merge the branch to the master branch

3. *Developer A* reviews the code on *Branch_C* and gives feedback to *Developer B*

4. *Developer B* modifies the code on *Branch_C* based on the feedback from *Developer A*

5. *Developer A* finally approves the change on *Branch_C* and merges it with the *master* branch

6. Developer B *sees* Developer A's *approval*

Note: For practice purposes, we are explaining several iterations between Developer A and Developer B. If you want to simply approve the change and merge the code, you can skip from step 3 onwards in this page and go to the next page.

1. Create a new feature on a new branch

At this step, *Developer B* creates *Branch_C* that diverges from the master branch and edits the HTML file as if she's writing code to create a new feature on the branch. Also, make some commits and push *Branch_C* to the Remote Repository.

Action by Developer B

First, create a new branch *Branch_C* from the master branch.

Command Line - INPUT

```
git checkout master
git checkout -b Branch_C
```

Action by Developer B

First, create a new branch *Branch_C* from the master branch.

Command Line - INPUT

```
git checkout master
git checkout -b Branch_C
```

Command Line - RESPONSE

```
Switched to a new branch 'Branch_C'
```

Edit the HTML file like shown below (add *<h1>C1LB</h1>* after *<!-- Branch C-->*).

C1LB indicates the following:

1. **C** - Branch_C
2. **1** - 1st commit
3. **L** - Committed in the Local Repository
4. **B** - Committed by *Developer B*.

git_remote_practice.html (Branch_C)

```
<!-- Branch C-->
<h1>C1LB</h1>
<!-- /Branch C-->
```

Commit the change with the commit message "*C1LB*" as shown below.

Command Line - INPUT

```
git commit -am "C1LB"
```

Command Line - RESPONSE

```
[Branch_C 7510fae] C1LB
1 file changed, 1 insertion(+), 1 deletion(-)
```

Repeat the same process of editing the file and committing the change twice.

Use *C2LB* and *C3LB* for each commit respectively and check the log to see the latest status.

Command Line - INPUT

```
git log --oneline
```

You can see that there are three new commits on *Branch_C*.

Command Line - RESPONSE

```
6fc9649 (HEAD -> Branch_C) C3LB
c33e4e8 C2LB
7510fae C1LB
4e7dbf9 (origin/master, origin/HEAD, master) M3LA
4e1a7d9 M2RA
4b30a1c M1LA
```

The HTML file status should look like the one below.

git_remote_practice.html (Branch_C)

```
<!-- Branch C-->
<h1>C1LB</h1>
<h1>C2LB</h1>
<h1>C3LB</h1>
<!-- /Branch C-->
```

Next, push *Branch_C* to the Remote Repository.

Command Line - INPUT

```
git push origin Branch_C
```

You can see that *Branch_C* is successfully pushed.

Now you can go to the next step.

2. Trigger a pull request to ask for review and merge

In this step, *Developer B* triggers a **pull request** to ask *Developer A* to review and merge the branch with the master branch.

Action by Developer B

1) When you push a branch to the Remote Repository, usually a message about the push is displayed on the Remote Repository site. To start creating a new pull request, click the **Compare & pull request button**.

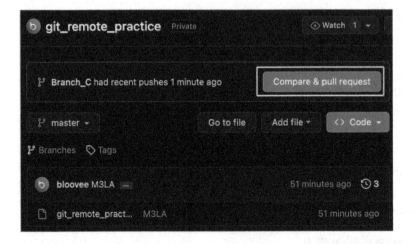

2) There are three main fields in the pull request form.

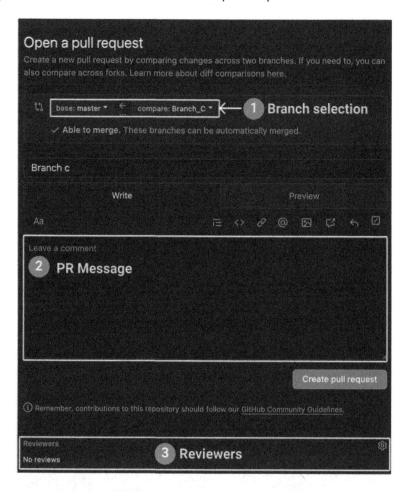

- **Branch selection**: You need to select a **base branch** and the **branch being merged** shown after "**compare**". In this case, *Developer B* selects the master branch for the base branch and *Branch_C* to compare.

- **Pull Request message** (PR message): typically, you need to describe what changes are to be made and why you are making the changes. You can use the editor provided and check its preview.

- **Reviewers**: You can select multiple reviewers. In this practice demonstration, we select *Developer A*: *bloovee*.

Once necessary fields are filled, click the **Create pull request** button to create the pull request.

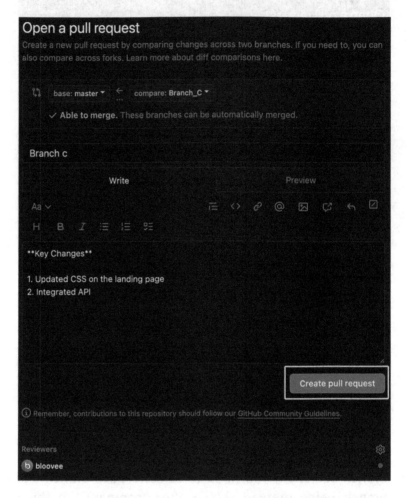

Note: There are other fields in the pull request form (e.g., setting milestones, assigning projects, etc.)

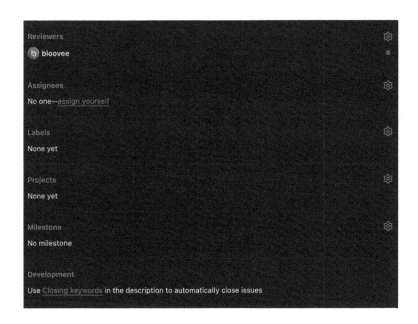

3. Review the code on the new branch and give feedback

At this step, *Developer A* reviews the code on *Branch_C* and gives feedback to *Developer B*.

Action by Developer A

1) When a pull request is generated, the repository owner and the reviewers receive an email notification like the one below. In this practice demo, *Developer A* is the owner and the reviewer. He receives two email notifications. In the email, you can find the link to the pull request. Click the link to go to the next step.

The email sent to the repository owner:

sky-blue2022 <notifications@github.com>
to bloovee/git_remote_practice, me, Review ▾

Key Changes

1. Updated CSS on the landing page
2. Integrated API

_____

You can view, comment on, or merge this pull request online at:

https://github.com/bloovee/git_remote_practice/pull/1

The email sent to reviewers:

sky-blue2022 <notifications@github.com>
to bloovee/git_remote_practice, me, Review ▾

@sky-blue2022 requested your review on: #1 Branch c.

Reply to this email directly, view it on GitHub, or unsubscribe.
You are receiving this because your review was requested.

2) On the pull request page, there are several tabs. The **Conversation** tab is the one which you need to look at first. It gives an overview of the pull request by showing the commit history and conversation logs.

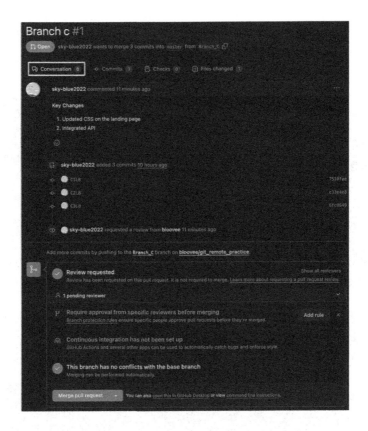

3) Another tab you need to check is the **Files changed** tab. In this tab, you can find the key changes committed by the requester (in this case, *Developer B*: *sky-blue2022*). As a reviewer, you can add review comments line by line before writing an overall review message. Click the **+** popup icon to open the comment field.

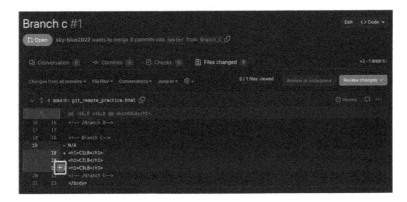

When you click the **Add single comment** button, the message immediately goes to the Conversation section so that other team members can see it.

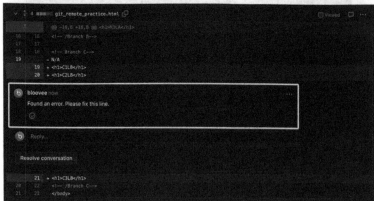

When you want to make a more comprehensive review, click the **Start a review** button.

4) After starting a review, you can continue to review line by line. When you are ready to finish the review, click the **Finish your review** button.

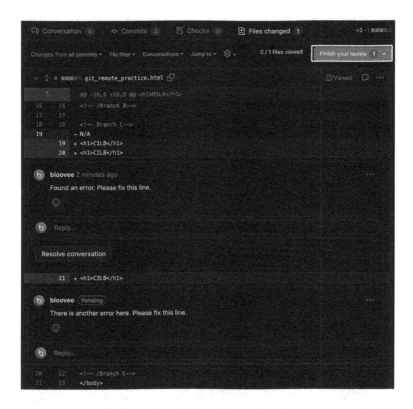

5) When you click the **Finish your review** button, the final review comment window pops up. You can write the final message and select one of the three types of review.

- **Comment**: submit general feedback without explicit approval
- **Approve**: submit feedback and approve merging these changes
- **Request changes**: submit feedback that must be addressed before merging

In the message, you can drag and drop a file to give a more detailed explanation. When you complete the message and select one of the options, click the **Submit review** button to finalize the review.

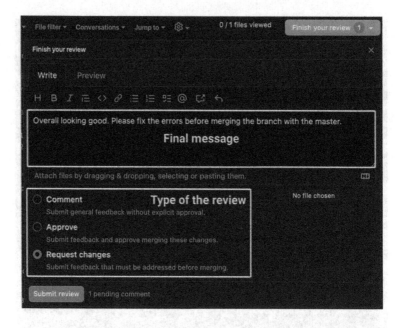

You can confirm that the changes have been requested.

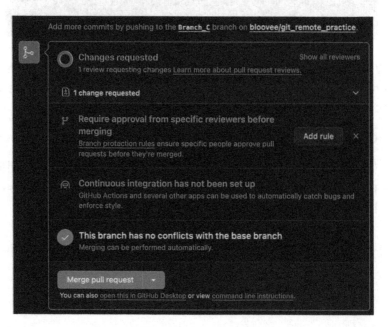

4. Modify the code and push it

In this step, *Developer B* modifies the code on *Branch_C* based on the feedback from *Developer A*.

Action by Developer B

1) When the reviewer completes the review, the requester (*Developer B* in this case) receives an email notification like the one below. Click the link to see the review comments in the Remote Repository.

2) You can view the review comments line by line in the browser like shown below.

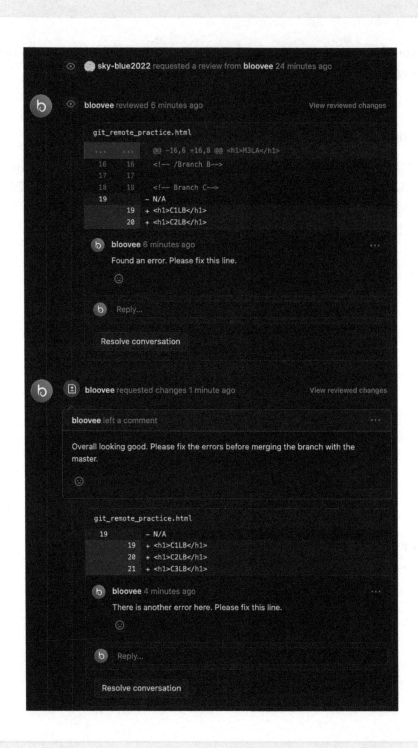

3) To fix the error, use the local text editor and the command line. Edit the file, make a commit, and push it to the Remote Repository as described below.

Before making an edit, make sure that you are running commands on *Branch_C*.

Command Line - INPUT

```
git checkout Branch_C
```

Command Line - RESPONSE

```
Already on 'Branch_C'
```

Edit the file as shown below: delete *C2LB* and add *C4LB*, and save the file.

git_remote_practice.html (Branch_C)

```
<!-- Branch C-->
<h1>C1LB</h1>

<h1>C3LB</h1>
<h1>C4LB</h1>
<!-- /Branch C-->
```

Commit the change and push the branch.

Command Line - INPUT

```
git commit -am "C4LB"
git push origin Branch_C
```

Command Line - RESPONSE

```
Enumerating objects: 5, done.
:
    6fc9649..3d69f7a Branch_C -> Branch_C
```

4) After pushing the branch, go to the Remote Repository.

You can see that the new commit has been pushed to the Remote Repository.

To ask for an approval, write comments to inform what you have done and press the **Comment** button to submit the comment.

5. Approve the edit

At this step, *Developer A* finally approves the change on *Branch_C* and merges it with the master branch.

Action by Developer A

1) When the requester (*Developer B*) resubmits the changes and comments, the reviewer (*Developer A*) receives an email notification like the one below. Click the link in the message or directly go to the Remote Repository.

 sky-blue2022 <notifications@github.com>
to Review, bloovee/git_remote_practice, me ▾

Already fixed the errors and pushed new code. Please review and merge the code.

—

Reply to this email directly, view it on GitHub or unsubscribe.
You are receiving this because your review was requested.

2) Go to the **Commits** tab to see the latest commit.

Merge Operation Using GitHub

Three approaches of Merge operation on Git Hub

Create a merge commit	Squash and merge	Rebase and merge

All commits from requested branch will be **merged to base branch** via merge commit

Commits from requested branch will be **combined into one commit** in the base branch

Commits from requested branch will be **rebased and merged to base branch**

Ɔ-libro

How to merge branches through the command line on the local computer was already explained in the previous chapter. In this section, we'll explain how to merge branches on the GitHub web platform.

The **merge** feature on GitHub gives similar functionality as the Git commands below. There are three merge approaches which are a combination of the three Git commands: the **git merge**, **git rebase**, and **git commit** commands.

> 1. Create a merge commit: **git merge --no-ff**
> 2. Squash and merge: **git merge --squash + git commit**
> 3. Rebase and merge: **git rebase + git merge**

1. Create a merge commit

This approach is the one most commonly used. According to this approach, the base branch captures and keeps all the commit histories from the topic branch as shown in the illustration on the left of the main figure.

2. Squash and merge

When you want to integrate all the small commits to simplify the commit history of the project, you can use this option. A drawback of this option is that all the commits of the topic branch are erased from the history as shown in the middle illustration on the main figure.

3. Rebase and merge

If you have many branches in the project and merge them into the *master* branch, the commit history of the project becomes very complex. This option is used to make the commit line straight as shown the illustration on the right of the main figure.

For a better understanding, please go through the following practice section.

Practice

Objective:
Learn the merge operations on the GitHub web platform

In this practice, we'll go through the three merge approaches on GitHub using the branches prepared on the previous pages. The target operations are illustrated below.

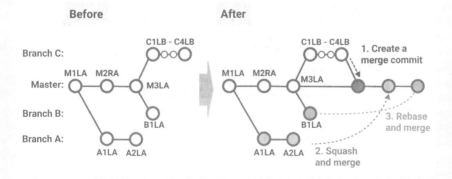

1. Create a merge commit: merge *Branch_C* into the *master* branch

2. Squash and merge: squash and merge *Branch_A*

3. Rebase and merge: rebase and merge *Branch_B*

1. Create a merge commit: merge Branch_C into the master branch

On the previous page, we have already explained about the pull request process until a reviewer approves the changes (*Developer A* already approved *Developer B*'s code).

The merge operation can be done by either party: the requester or the approver of the pull request. In this step, we'll explain the case where the reviewer (*Developer A*) conducts the merge operation.

Action by Developer A

1) To execute the merge operation, go to the pull request page created on the previous page. Select **Create a merge commit** in the **Merge pull request** pull-down and click the button again.

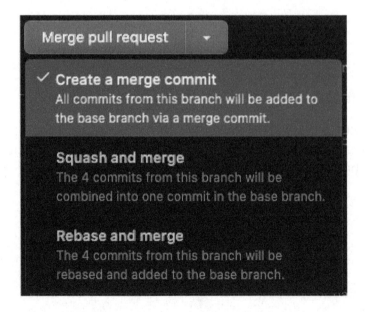

2) Press the **Confirm merge** button to execute.

3) A confirmation message is displayed:

4) Check the commit history on the *master* branch. Go to the **Code** tab and open the commits.

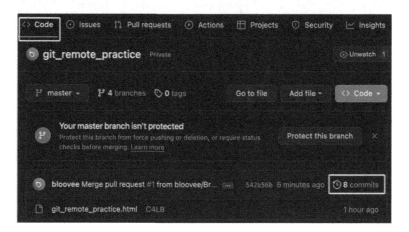

You will see that *Branch_C* was integrated into the *master* branch while the commits made on *Branch_C* were kept unchanged.

2. Squash and merge: squash and merge Branch_A

In this step, we'll continue to execute the merge operation with the *Developer A* account. When you want to execute the merge operation by yourself, you can create a pull request on your own and execute the merge operation.

Action by Developer A

1) Create a new pull request from the **Pull requests** tab and press the **New pull requests** button.

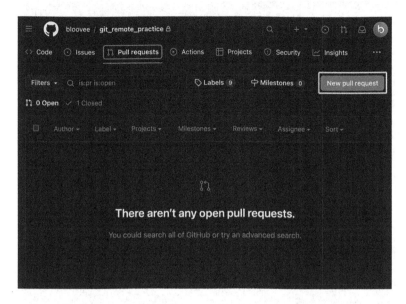

2) Select *Branch_A* to compare, and press the **Create pull request** button

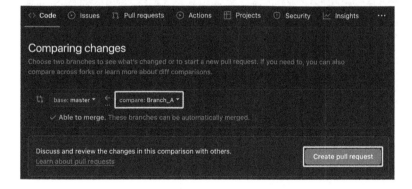

3) Add a **PR comment** and press the **Create pull request** button. As *Developer A* executes the merge operation himself, you don't need to select a reviewer.

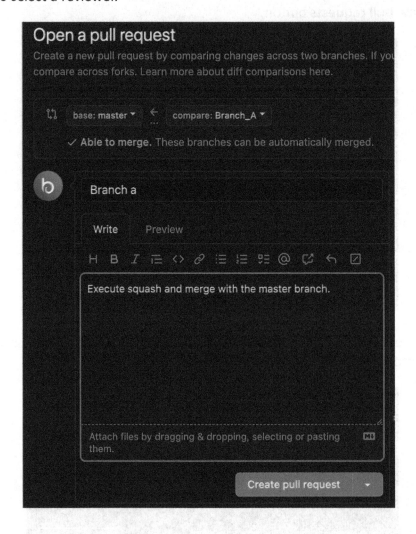

4) Select **Squash and merge** under the **Merge pull request** pull-down.

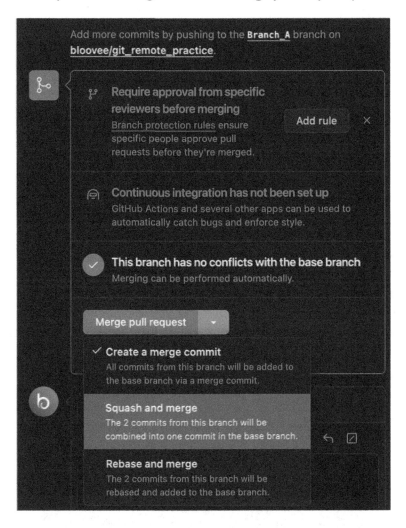

5) Press the **Confirm squash and merge** button. The squash merge is executed.

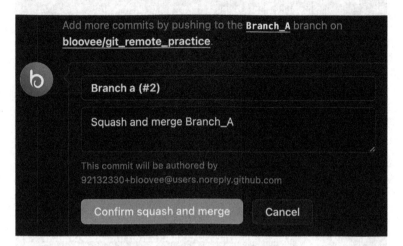

6) Check the commit history on the *master* branch. You can see that *Branch_A* was squashed and merged. As the original commits are squashed, you cannot see the original commit details (*A1LA, A2LA*).

3. Rebase and merge: rebase and merge Branch_B

Finally, execute rebase and merge *Branch_B*. We continue the operation using *Developer A's* account.

1) Follow the same process as in the previous step until the merge option selection (creating a pull request comparing the *master* branch with *Branch_B*).

For the merge operation, select **Rebase and merge** in the merge option list.

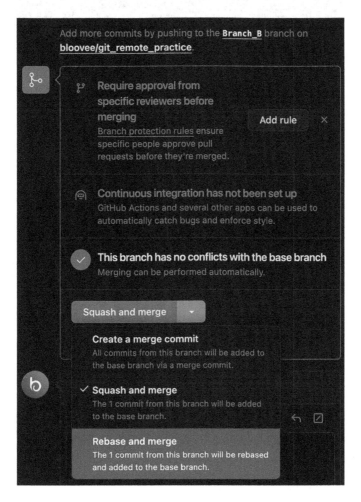

2) Press the Confirm rebase and merge button. Rebase and merge are executed.

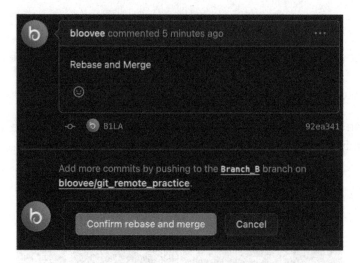

3) Check the commit history on the *master* branch. You can see that *Branch_B* was rebased and merged - commit *B1LA* became the *HEAD* of the *master* branch.

4. Update the local branches

All the operations in this page were made on the GitHub platform through the web browser. The changes have not been synchronized in the Local Repositories. In this step, synchronize the changes made on the Remote Repository with *Developer A* and *Developer B*'s Local Repositories.

Action by Developer A

First, check the latest status of the *master* branch. You can see that the branch has not been updated yet.

Command Line - INPUT

```
git checkout master
git log --oneline
```

Command Line - RESPONSE

```
4e7dbf9 (HEAD -> master, origin/master) M3LA
4e1a7d9 M2RA
4b30a1c M1LA
```

Run the pull command and check the log with the **--graph** option to see the latest commit tree.

Command Line - INPUT

```
git pull origin master
git log --oneline --graph
```

```
* 231b752 (HEAD -> master, origin/master) B1LA
* 6ae3208 Branch a (#2)
* 542b56b Merge pull request #1 from bloovee/Branch_C
|\
| * 3d69f7a C4LB
| * 6fc9649 C3LB
| * c33e4e8 C2LB
| * 7510fae C1LB
|/
* 4e7dbf9 M3LA
* 4e1a7d9 M2RA
* 4b30a1c M1LA
```

Repeat the same process for *Developer B*.

Action by Developer B

First, check the latest status of the *master* branch. You can see that the branch has not been updated yet.

```
git checkout master
git log --oneline
```

```
4e7dbf9 (HEAD -> master, origin/master, origin/HEAD) M3LA
4e1a7d9 M2RA
4b30a1c M1LA
```

Run the pull command and check the log with the **--graph** option to see the latest commit tree.

Command Line - INPUT

```
git pull origin master
git log --oneline --graph
```

Command Line - RESPONSE

```
* 231b752 (HEAD -> master, origin/master, origin/HEAD) B1LA
* 6ae3208 Branch a (#2)
* 542b56b Merge pull request #1 from bloovee/Branch_C
|\
| * 3d69f7a (origin/Branch_C, Branch_C) C4LB
| * 6fc9649 C3LB
| * c33e4e8 C2LB
| * 7510fae C1LB
|/
* 4e7dbf9 M3LA
* 4e1a7d9 M2RA
* 4b30a1c M1LA
```

The demo code is available in this repository (**Demo Code**[1]).

---

1 https://github.com/git-github-introduction/git_remote_practice

Chapter 7

Supplemental Topics

To master the Git and GitHub operations, you need to understand key commands, key features, and some technical terms. GitHub also provides more useful features that have not yet been explained in this course.

In this chapter, we'll cover the following supplemental topics for Git & GitHub Introduction.

TOPICS

1. Git Key Commands and GitHub Key Features

2. Git & GitHub Glossary

3. GitHub Other Features

Git Key Commands and GitHub Key Features

Initial Settings	
$ git config	register username, email, text editor, etc.

Launch Project	
$ git init	create new local repository under current directory
$ git clone [URL]	bring remote branch to local computer
Fork	create replica of existing repository on GitHub

Edit & Commit	
$ git add [file path]	add working files to staging area
$ git status	show status of working tree and staging area
$ git commit	record files in staging area to the local respository
$ git log	show commit histories of current branch
$ git diff	show differences of working tree, INDEX and commits
$ git restore [file path]	update working tree with latest commit
$ git rm [file path]	remove file from the working tree and stage status
$ git reset [commit]	reverse commit histories

Work with Branches	
$ git branch [branch name]	create new branch
$ git branch	list up branches in local repository
$ git checkout / $ git switch	switch branches
$ git merge [branch]	merge branches
$ git rebase [branch]	move diverged point to HEAD of base branch
$ git stash	temporaliry store working tree and INDEX

Remote Collaboration	
$ git remote add origin [URL]	create link between remote repository and local repository
$ git push origin [branch name]	upload commit histories to remote repository from local
$ git pull origin [branch name]	get remote branch data and merge with local branch
$ git fetch origin	get remote branch data
Pull Request	create request to review and merge
Merge	merge branches on GitHub

This page summarizes the key Git commands and key GitHub features covered in this course. You can use this page as a cheat sheet.

Chapter 2. Git & GitHub Initial Settings

$ git config: a command used when you register (or change) key user settings in the Git system. For example, you can do the following with this command

- Register your username and email address
- Register a text editor
- Check configured settings
- Clear configured settings

Chapter 3. Git & GitHub Project Setup

$ git init: a command used for initiating a Git project by creating a new Local Repository in the current directory.

$ git clone: a command used to create a link to a Remote Repository and bring the project directory from the Remote Repository with commit histories to your local computer. This command is used only the first time you bring the project directory to your local computer. The **git clone** command establishes a connection between the Remote Repository and your local computer by registering on your computer the URL that defines the location of the Remote Repository. Once the connection is established, you can **Pull** or **Fetch** the Remote Repository.

Fork: a feature provided by GitHub and used to create a replica of a Remote Repository on GitHub. After implementing Fork, the replicated repository will be separated from the original repository. You can modify codes in the replicated repository on your own without permission from the owners of the original repository (within the software license agreement, if any). Fork is not a git command. It is executed on the GitHub website. Go to the GitHub site and find the repository which you want to create a replica of. There is a Fork button on the Remote Repository page. Press the Fork button to implement Fork.

Chapter 4. Edit & Commit

$ git add: with this command, you can add files to the *Staging Area* (INDEX), where you can prepare and check files before registering in your Local Repository.

$ git status: with this command, you can see the status of the *Working Tree* (working directory) and the *Staging Area* (INDEX). This status lets you see which changes have been staged, which haven't, and which files aren't being tracked by Git.

$ git commit: with this command, you can register files in your Local Repository. Once the files are registered, you can retrieve the saved version of the set of files at any time.

$ git log: with this command, you can check the information on the commit history of the repository

$ git diff: with this command, you can check differences between the *Working Tree*, *Staging Area* (*INDEX*), and commit histories.

$ git restore: with this command, you can bring your *Working Tree* back to the latest commit or a specific commit. This command is useful when you want to clear your edits and go back to a cleaner version.

$ git rm: with this command, you can delete files or directories under the *Working Tree* and the *Staging Area* (*INDEX*). When you want to reflect the deleted status as a formal version, you need to create another commit.

$ git reset: with this command, you can reset the *Staging Area* (*INDEX*) or change commit histories with or without changing the contents of your local files.

Chapter 5. Work With Branches

$ git branch: this command is a multi-use command. For example, it is used for creating a new branch, checking branch status, and deleting an unused branch.

$ git checkout: with this command, you can switch your current branch to a selected branch.

$ git switch: with this command, you can get the same result as that of **git checkout**. It is a command newly introduced as a substitute for the **git checkout** command.

$ git merge: with this command, you can merge branches. The merge operation can be done through a Remote Repository on the GitHub website.

$ git rebase: with this command, you can reapply commits on top of another base branch. This command is useful when you want to streamline commits that diverged into multiple branches. The rebase operation can also be done through a Remote Repository on the GitHub website. It is an option of the merge feature of GitHub.

$ git stash: with this command, you can separately manage WIP (Work In Progress) codes. When you want to switch the current branch in the middle of editing the *Working Tree*, the edits can prevent you from switching the current branch. In that case, this command is useful. The stashed lines of code are parked somewhere temporarily.

Chapter 6. Remote Collaboration

$ git remote: this command is a multi-use command relating to managing a Remote Repository. For example, with the **git remote add** command, you can establish a link between a Remote Repository and a Local Repository. The **git remote -v** command shows the status of the link.

$ git push: with this command, you can upload project directories and files along with commit histories for a specified branch from your computer to a Remote Repository

$ git pull: with this command, you can download project directories and files along with commit histories for a specified branch from a Remote Repository. This command also merges the downloaded branch with an existing branch under the Local Repository.

$ git fetch: with this command, you can obtain the latest Remote Repository information and store it on your local computer. This command doesn't enforce merging branches in the Local Repository. If you want to update the Local Repository, you need to run the **git merge** or **git checkout** command.

Pull request: this feature is used to ask a reviewer to review your edits. It is especially useful when you want to ask the reviewer to merge your branch (a topic branch) with the main branch (e.g., master branch).

Merge: this feature gives similar functionality as the **git merge** command and the **git rebase** command. You can execute merge or rebase operations on the GitHub website. There are three merge approaches. 1) Create a merge commit, 2) Squash and merge, 3) Rebase and merge.

GLOSSARY

There are several technical terms for Git and GitHub. This provides a glossary of the Git and GitHub key terminologies.

B

Branch: an independent line of development with a commit history. Different branches give a different registration space; each branch has its own coding history (a line of commits).

C

Clone: an action that brings a project directory from a Remote Repository with commit histories to the local computer.

Commit: a snapshot that records the status of coding in repositories.

Commit hash: a unique ID of each commit. When you want to retrieve a commit, you need this hash.

Conflict: a situation when two developers edit the same lines of code in the same file.

F

Fast-forward merge: a merge action that doesn't create a new commit. It simply advances the *HEAD* of the current branch by incorporating another branch.

Fetch: an action that updates the remote-tracking branch status. It brings the latest Remote Repository status onto the local computer.

Fork: a feature provided by GitHub and used to create a replica of a Remote Repository on GitHub.

G

.gitignore file: a text file that tells the Git system which files or directories to ignore when tracking files and directories.

H

HEAD: a pointer to the last commit in the current checkout branch.

HTTPS: Hypertext Transfer Protocol Secure. It is an extension of HTTP used to build a more secure network.

I

INDEX: Staging Area. A buffer area used to prepare working files for commit.

L

Local Repository: a local computer repository where committed files are stored with version histories

M

Master Branch: a branch used as a master of a project's coding activity. The master branch is the default branch until you create a new branch for your project.

Merge: an action for integrating branches.

N

Non-Fast-forward merge: a merge action that creates a new commit. The merge action is recorded as one commit.

O

Origin: a standard Remote Repository name. When you clone a Remote Repository, the default Remote Repository name is origin.

P

PAT: Personal Access Token generated on the GitHub website. It is used as a password to access Remote Repositories.

Pull Request: a request to review changes on a topic branch and merge it with a main branch (e.g., the master branch).

Pull: an action that downloads the latest Remote Repository information and merges with one of the existing branches in the Local Repository.

Push: an action that uploads a branch in the Local Repository to the Remote Repository.

R

Rebase: an action that changes the divergence point to the latest commit of the base branch.

Remote Repository: a repository where committed files are stored on the web and can be shared with others.

Remote-tracking branch: a branch that tracks a Remote Repository from the Local Repository (e.g., origin/master, origin/Branch_A).

S

SSH: Secure Shell Protocol. It is typically used for remote access to servers or computers.

Staging Area: a buffer area used to prepare working files for commit. It is also called INDEX.

T

Topic Branch: a branch used to work on coding separate from the main lines of coding activities. It is used to add a new feature or fix bugs. It is also called a feature branch.

U

Upstream branch: the Remote Repository tracked by the remote-tracking branch.

W

Working Tree: working directories and files that you can edit.

GitHub Other Features

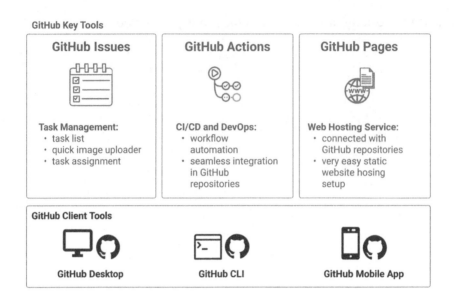

GitHub Key Tools

GitHub Issues	GitHub Actions	GitHub Pages
Task Management:	**CI/CD and DevOps:**	**Web Hosting Service:**
• task list	• workflow automation	• connected with GitHub repositories
• quick image uploader	• seamless integration in GitHub repositories	• very easy static website hosing setup
• task assignment		

GitHub Client Tools

GitHub Desktop   GitHub CLI   GitHub Mobile App

GitHub is no longer just a Git hosting service. There are several features and client tools that you can use even with a free plan. Here are some examples.

Features

GitHub Issues is a task management tool. GitHub users can easily create project task lists using GitHub Issues. You can upload images by simply dragging & dropping them and easily add images to the issue list. GitHub Issues is a powerful tool for communicating with your team members effectively. You can also assign your team members to each task.

GitHub Actions is a tool used to support CI/CD and DevOps workflow. Even before GitHub Actions was introduced, GitHub was a popular platform for CI/CD and DevOps through API, connecting with other applications such as CircleCI, Travis CI, and Jenkins. GitHub Actions give you more opportunities to improve your workflow within your repositories on GitHub.

GitHub Pages is a website hosting service provided by GitHub. GitHub Pages is connected with GitHub repositories. You can publish website documents stored in a GitHub repository very easily. You can check this link **GitHub Pages**[1] for more details.

---

1 https://d-libro.com/topic/github-pages/

GitHub also provides other tools and services like auto security alerts using **Dependabot** and AI developer tool **GitHub Copilot**.

Client Tools

Several client tools are also available to improve your working efficiencies.

GitHub Desktop is used for controlling GitHub on a local GUI application.

GitHub CLI is used for controlling GitHub from the local computer's command line.

GitHub Mobile App provides a mobile user interface to easily check the status of issues and repositories.

About D-Libro

https://d-libro.com/

D-Libro is a learning platform and eBook library specialized in digital skills, including:

- Programming and coding
- Web and application design
- Cloud-based infrastructure management
- Digital Marketing

Git & GitHub Introduction

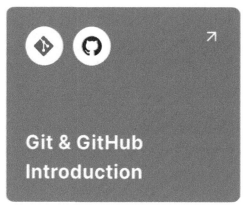

https://d-libro.com/course/git-github-introduction/

Linux Introduction

https://d-libro.com/course/linux-introduction/

HTML & CSS Introduction

https://d-libro.com/course/html-css-introduction/

Django Introduction

https://d-libro.com/course/django-introduction/

There are several courses available for beginners.

SEO Tutorial for Beginners

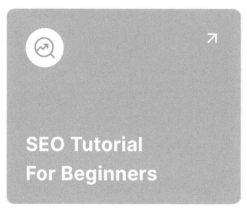

https://d-libro.com/course/seo-tutorial-for-beginners/

Made in United States
Orlando, FL
25 November 2024

54381146R00226